WE WERE BRAVE

A Collection of Short Stories

written by

our own Vietnam Veterans

"Never tell a soldier he does not know the cost of war." - Lt. General Frank Benson

The last spoken line in the movie *Eye in the Sky* played by Alan Rickman, his last performance.

We Were Brave

This publication is a work of non-fiction. The views expressed in this collection are solely by the authors and do not necessarily represent the views of the publisher or the editor, who both hereby disclaim any responsibility for them.

HEADIN' HOME

There was an awareness both day and night
That you weren't a veteran 'til you made the flight,
And it was a long time coming.

Then it finally arrived, the day we were all hoping for,
The day to step off the distant shore
Of South Viet Nam.
And step onto that "Giant Bird" and scream away
Headin' home again.

My vision or dream,
And I think this was shared
With others that were there,
Was to scream away at high noon
So I could turn and stare,
At Viet Nam behind me.

But it wasn't a day flight.
In darkness we left.
Just got aboard and flew away,
Feeling like thieves in the night.

I say thieves and I say it willing.
The takeoff was almost chilling.
It was quiet and austere,
And no one dare make a sound.
It was a silent moment of care
For our friends we left on the ground.
You'd think we'd be cheering
To be young and alive and free and
Headin' home,
Instead we were praying
That our friends would survive
To get a flight of their own.

But we'd never know
And it's like we stole something they might need,
Fighting support or fellowship,
In the event that they might bleed.
I think this was shared,
In unison we stared from the flying bus,
And as hard as we stared
We could not see, Vietnam behind us.

But we were alive and lucky and on a flight,
And proceeded on into the night.. .
Headin' home.. .

Dennis Sprague
1/502-1969-1970

CONTENTS

ACKNOWLEDGMENTS

I became passionate about this project after reading some stories written by a former alumnus from my school. Then one day enjoying lunch with some graduates from Clermont High and knowing how many young men from our community served in Vietnam, the idea of putting together a collection of short stories written by our own veterans was born.

The contributors of these stories are not writers. They were young men caught in a controversial war. After receiving their draft notices most enlisted to serve their country, a country that failed to show them due respect upon their return, scarring some of them even more than the scars they received in the war. Some were lucky, some were not, but like their willingness to serve, a few have shared their stories for a good cause—the funding of an educational scholarship.

Below is a list of individuals whom I want to acknowledge and thank for their participation with the writing of this book...W*e Were Brave.*

Thank you, Patrick McCrary, for sharing with me the stories you wrote about your experience in Vietnam. Your stories were the inspiration behind the creation of this book spurred on by three loyal Clermont

Alumni: Sharon Prescott Jenkins, Patty Lucas Green and her sister, Debbie Lucas Wharton.

A special thank you to Patty, who set about collecting names of those from our school who served in Vietnam. Initially, thirteen men made up the list, but with John Hotaling's help and numerous posts on the Highlander site, the list grew to forty-eight names. Thank you, John.

Next, I want to thank the team members of my local critique group, who at first were unsure about critiquing stories written by men who were not writers. Nonetheless, once they started reading the stories, their devotion to this project grew. Thank you, Jim, Melita, Laurie, Lynn and Chris for offering feedback that helped to enrich these stories. And a very special thank you to Jim, who he himself served in Vietnam and was a big help in getting those all-important military details accurate.

Then there is our own editor in chief, Laurie. Besides critiquing, she designed the cover and formatted the book for publication, while working full-time and pursuing her own writing career. In addition, she donated her service. Love you Laurie. You are the best.

I would also like to thank another alumnus Marsha McAllister Parlow, a 1965 graduate of Clermont High. Marsha volunteered to help some of the reluctant contributors. She did this by meeting with the men, recording their stories, writing them up, and then met with them again before sending the written version to me. Thanks to her efforts, we were able to collect enough submissions to make this project a reality.

Finally, my biggest heartfelt "thank you" goes to our veterans, along with three non-military women, who shared their stories. Even though most of the contributing individuals had little experience as writers, they did an incredible job. Some accounts revolve around the devastation of war, up close and personal. A few share comical experiences, awarding readers a chance to breathe and laugh, while others wrote thought provoking moments. Then there were those who provided stories giving a different perspective—a look inside the mind of these young soldiers scarred by what they saw and had to do. You guys and ladies did an awesome job, and I am so proud of each one of you.

Sincerely,
M.C. Brown (Mary Collins Brown)

INTRODUCTION

We Were Brave

A Collection of Short Stories written by our
own Vietnam Veterans

by M.C. Brown

The collection of narratives within is the
result of my reading several stories written
by a former Clermont High School student,
who served during the Vietnam era. Since
the early seventies, I had given little thought
to that time—a time filled with controversy
due to the war. It wasn't until I began reading
this man's stories that the war became real
to me. Before, I had been nothing more
than a casual observer, never giving any
thought to what these brave soldiers endured.

1

Forty-eight young men from Clermont, Florida, and maybe more, left the safety of our community to fight in a war fraught by protest. Those men went off to Vietnam with mixed emotions. Some were drafted, others joined, and when they left—none of them knew if they would come back alive.

Our community was one of the lucky ones; we did not lose a single man. Nonetheless, in all this time, did anyone give thought to how these men must have felt or what they suffered upon their return home?

Many young soldiers found themselves spat upon, dodging objects thrown at them, and some even endured people yelling cruel obscenities, such as calling them baby killers. No one seemed aware that many of these men were mere babes themselves, some as young as seventeen, returning with enough emotional baggage to last a lifetime.

Even today, there are those who still bear the scars of the Vietnam War. Some display physical scars, while others carry emotional and mental scars as they struggle to forget what they did and what they saw. Some came back feeling ashamed for their part in the war.

Those spared the horror of face-to-face combat were the lucky ones. Their stories will serve to lighten the devastating effects of that period of history.

In this collection of narratives, journey with the authors who survived the war. Many ignite the senses with descriptions of pain and images of terror, while holding on to the hope of returning home alive with all body parts intact.

It is my sincere hope for the contributors telling of the carnage that writing their stories might serve as a healing tool for them—a chance to unleash memories that have haunted them over the years.

As for the reader, may this book help bring about a better understanding and a sense of pride for those who went, fought, and returned.

EDITORIAL ESSAY

THE VIETNAM WAR
...that should never have been

by Joe Koester

Colonial powers once meant greatness, strength, prestige and a host of other superlatives. In reality, it meant imposing the will of a stronger nation on a lesser one. History is replete with examples of colonialisms, and we, here in the United States, are evidence of its failure. The colonies rebelled and it ended with the defeat of the mighty British Army at Yorktown and the birth of a free nation. History does repeat itself.

We seldom learn from our mistakes. The French and other earlier invaders were no different. Colonialism was an opportunity to bring an enlightened civilization to countries who, in some cases, were little better than savages. More often than not, however, the indigenous people prevailed over the invading or intruding foreigners. The Vietnam War was no different from any of the above mentioned with many to follow. Iraq and Afghanistan are examples of more recent wars.

The French colonized Vietnam and introduced a new and refined culture, railroads, infrastructure, a modern and beautiful language as well as many other tangibles and intangibles. However, they failed to understand that the Vietnamese culture predated theirs and defeated a number of other interlopers long before the French arrived on the scene.

The locals took issue with these new European intruders and after many years of strife, the French faced another Waterloo at Dien Bien Phu in 1954. When the French appealed for help from the United States, they were rebuffed and left disgraced and defeated.

Fast forward a number of years and the United States became locked in a "Cold War" with the communists, led by the mighty Union of Soviet Socialist Republics (USSR), known as our foe with their on again—off again ally Red China or the Chinese Communists.

The U.S. was concerned about the spread of communism, and the need to stop it wherever it appeared to be gaining ground. Following the enormous losses Russia and the Soviet Union sustained in World War II, Soviet leader Joseph Stalin wanted to establish a buffer zone around his country as a guarantee that nobody could attack them again without warning as Adolf Hitler had done in 1941. Therefore, Stalin gobbled up the countries of Eastern Europe as a buffer zone; thus, the spread of communism over a large portion of Europe following World War II.

This was of great concern for the United States and its allies. They needed to ensure that communism could be held in check. We had seen it take hold in China following the Great War, and then in nearby North Korea. The future great Vietnamese Leader, Ho Chi Minh, had been rebuffed by the U.S. sowing the seeds for a further spread of communism.

The Geneva agreement of 1954 split Vietnam along the 17th parallel and two new countries were formed, much like the Koreas, in this case North and South Vietnam, Communist North and "Free" South. Another line drawn in the sand, and like Korea, two more countries divided into

North and South, reminiscent our own country many years ago.

A fear of falling dominoes developed. Touch the first one and the remainder all fall in a long line. Now, in Southeast Asia, a communist front emerged in the north, consisting of China and North Vietnam. The dominoes were poised to fall.

The United States supported the "free and democratic" South Vietnam, determined to stop the threat of communism at the 17th parallel dividing the two Vietnams. Sound familiar? There is another DMZ further north, dividing the two Koreas at the 38th parallel of latitude.

Our country took a stand to thwart the potential fall of dominoes representing South Vietnam, Laos, Cambodia, Thailand, Malaysia, Burma and beyond. Backing the government of the Republic of South Vietnam, President John F. Kennedy agreed that there was a need to send in advisors to help train the Army of the Republic of South Vietnam (ARVN) to defend itself from the communist threat north and beyond.

Under President Lyndon Johnson, our presence grew from a handful of advisors to reconnaissance elements, air units for close air support, naval support, a swiftly growing logistical infrastructure and the introduction of combat troops in 1965.

Once we had a foothold, our presence grew exponentially and by 1968 we had over a half million troops in-country engaging in combat. There was also bombing of the north and supply routes in neighboring Laos and Cambodia. Our efforts to stop the dominoes now engulfed all of Southeast Asia.

History has many examples of an occupying army failing and greater forces beaten by a much lesser force. The superior foreign force has fixed structures and installations, those vastly mobile and smaller forces do not. They pick the time and place of their attacks, usually on the fixed installations of the foreign forces. This strategy called guerrilla warfare usually prevails. It triumphed in the American Revolution, the French Revolution, the fall of the Roman Empire, and in Vietnam. We should have learned from history—the recipe for disaster written on the wall. Nevertheless, like Napoleon, we needed to experience our Waterloo in Vietnam and later in a couple of other places. Though our intentions might have been honorable and our desire to spread our democratic form of government noble, it didn't matter— the Vietnam War was doomed to failure.

Sadly, the United States and our foes never realized this until it was far too late, with an enormous cost in lives on both sides, and squandered treasure. Perhaps one small glimmer of hope and good came from all of this carnage. We can only hope that all the players, great and small, begin to see the futility of a third World War, and the destruction and holocaust should another take place. The men and women who answered the call and served in the Vietnam War or the American War as the Vietnamese called it, served bravely and valiantly, and deserved better treatment than they received when they returned home. These are their stories, and we dedicate this collection to these patriots and heroes.

COMPASSION IN WAR

Kill them when we have to, but save them
when we can

by Patrick McCrary

I recall a time in my Vietnam tour when
the causality was not one of our men or
one of theirs, but a woman. At this point in
history, only men were allowed to engage in
combat actions, at least on our side. You
had to be tough as nails emotionally as
well as physically fit to endure such a test
of human will.

The murderous consequences of combat
are best endured by men without feelings
of compassion. Shocking, you may say, but
it is probably true for most military outfits.
In the midst of all the death, destruction,

and blood and guts witnessed in war, stands the United States Marine Corps. We were trained killers and compassion was somewhere in the very back of the manual.

During one of our many patrols in the "Arizona Territory" of the An Hoa basin, we stumbled across a wide trail that led from the mountains, due north of the An Hoa combat base. The trail was not on our maps.

The maps we used were very good. Almost every trail—small, medium and large, and every village with individual hoochs was shown on the maps. Finding a trail as large and wide as this was a surprise to everyone and scary to me. It meant we would have to investigate, search and find the origin and the purpose of this unknown road.

The first patrol went out in mid-afternoon. They returned several hours later reporting the trail curved and wound its way into the mountains. The road was well-used and showed signs of recent use. Our C.O. sent several patrols up the trail that night after our rifle company set up a defensive perimeter at the base of the mountains.

At daybreak, when the last group returned with no contact, our rifle company was ordered to set a company-sized ambush from the side of a mountain that overlooked the trail. The jungle canopy was thick and it took some time for each fire team to find a suitable spot with a clear field of fire.

I found this a welcomed bit of reprieve— no long patrols in the stifling heat, no moving into villages unannounced. Just lie on the side of a mountain and let the war go by. One man watched, one man relaxed, but as it so often happens in war, the enemy shows up.

We waited after their point man walked into our killing zone, allowing as many of them as possible to enter. When we received the order—we fired. Our position was 100 meters above them. The mixture of M-16 rifle, M-60 machine gun and M-79 grenade fire was devastating. The enemy began their disappearing act as we scrambled down the mountainside almost at a charge. I don't think they fired one round in response to our ambush. We found several of the North Vietnam Army (NVA) dead along with blood trails leading into the mountains. The NVA and the Viet Cong (VC) seemed to be able to melt into the jungle.

Although we had dealt a hard blow to them, there was one shocking discovery—a beautiful woman in her mid-twenties, most likely serving as a nurse, quivering with fright. Slim, well-kept and fed, she'd been shot through the leg and the stomach. She was either unable or unwilling to flee with the rest of the wounded enemy.

Our corpsman tended to her wounds and determined she could survive with immediate medical attention. We radioed for a medical evacuation helicopter. It would be difficult as well as dangerous to evacuate a Marine, but to some of us, to evacuate the enemy was nuts. Here we were, in a canopy jungle, in a valley in the mountains—a C46 helicopter was not gonna find a place to land. Period.

As the Sea Knight approached, we marked our position in the jungle with a smoke grenade. The Marine pilot brought his craft to a hover just above us and the crew chief began to lower a "dead man's sling" down. This item is like a noose, large enough to fit over your head and around your body. It is designed to fit under your armpits, while you lock your arms together as best you can. The crew chief then winches you into the waiting chopper. Great invention, yes, unless you are shot or frozen with terror.

We tried several times to give instructions to the woman on what she needed to do. With each attempt, she wouldn't even get off the ground a few feet before slipping out of the sling. I thought she might die right here with her friends.

Now, about the compassion I spoke of earlier...With disregard for his own safety, one of my fellow squad members removed the noose from the enemy, slipped it under his own armpits, gently cradled the woman in his arms, looked into my eyes and nodded his head, "take us up."

I gave the crew chief thumbs up and he started the winch.

The Marine piloting that aircraft was a master of his machine. He kept that C46 hovering over us for nearly 30 minutes. The problem with a winch and cable is that the cable can get twisted. I stood in horror, unable to move, as the cable began to unwind and put a brave Marine and his human cargo into a high-speed spin. At the height they were now, a fall would surely be fatal. To ensure his safety, all he needed to do was release her. Nevertheless, he held onto the wounded woman as the winch slowly pulled them closer to the aircraft.

Knowing he must be tiring, I began to pray for the operation to go faster. I could hardly contain myself when the cable finally wound all the way to the aircraft and the crew chief hauled both of them inside the C46. I found myself hoping the pilot would pull out and take my friend with him for a day's rest. However, the compassion he had for the woman changed to wanting to be back with his squad.

I watched as he put the sling back over his head and signaled the crew chief to lower him. When he touched the ground, our eyes met. I couldn't help but smile at him as we both let out a deep sigh of relief. I handed him his M-16 as the Marine pilot flew his aircraft out of the valley and out of our sight. A lump formed in my throat as I looked around us at the dead enemy and the thoughts of the morning's events raced in my mind. I said to him, "You know, you just saved that woman's life. I don't think anyone else would have done that."

"Maybe you're right, Mac, but she is, after all, a human being. Kill them when we have to, but save them when we can."

I'm sure the Marine Corps has had many men like him in our glorious history.

However, I never met them, but Lance Corporal Stukensmit brought to life the line in our hymn "And to keep our honor clean." He made all Marines, past, present, and future, proud. To this day, when our hymn is played and I hear those words, my heart swells with pride. It stirs my memory back to that terrible time and of the compassion shown by that Marine.

I pray for our great country and give thanks that there are still great men like him, who are willing to put compassion for others before their own well-being. And, I give thanks that there are still United

States Marines who "kill them when they have to, but save them when they can." God Bless the Marine Corps.

THE MAKING OF
A MAN NAMED JOE

by Joe Koester

I am a conservative by nature and turned twenty-one while in the Air Force. Uninformed about politics when the opportunity came to vote, my first vote was for Barry Goldwater. I wanted to register as an Independent, for my feelings were somewhere between the rhetoric of the two opposing parties. Then, I discovered I couldn't vote in the primaries, so I changed to Republican because I was more closely aligned with the conservative viewpoint, and I suppose that's where I still am today.

When I was in the service (1960 to 1964), my country was at war, and I believed in the domino theory, and supported what we were trying to do.

Following my four-year stint, I took a position with the National Security Agency in 1966. A wise old Navy chief I worked with tried to dissuade my views about Vietnam but couldn't. I found out the agency was sending people to Vietnam to provide intelligence support to the military. I applied for a position, was accepted, trained in the target area back at HQ, and left for my assignment in Vietnam.

One of the nice things about being in the intelligence business is that a person has a lot of information available. I was an analyst by nature with over four years' experience, so I looked at a lot of information. Also, I traveled a great deal. I visited a prison run by the South Vietnam Army and saw the metal cages where they held the VC. They weren't tall enough for them to stand. That was when I began to doubt the rationale and reasons given for our presence and involvement.

Strangely enough, my desire to do my job to the best of my ability did not change. Our government was wrong to be there; it wasn't going to have a good ending. Yet, I did my best to provide the information to kill the enemy and to protect our troops. Weird huh?

After I had been in the country for perhaps three months, a seminal event occurred one morning following a long night at work. I had a large motor scooter, a Japanese Rabbit that I drove to and from work rather than using a military van. I figured it was safer than being in a marked car, and more convenient.

That morning, my good friend and fellow coworker, Jim Springer, and I were heading down Plantation Road from Military Assistance Command Vietnam Headquarters (MACV HQ) to our Bachelor Officer's Quarters in Cholon (Chinese part of Saigon). Low on fuel, I pulled into a service station. As I was finishing filling the tank, we heard an explosion, which was not all that unusual.

We headed down the road but didn't get far. Traffic, which consisted of motor cycles, bikes, trucks, etc., had pretty much stopped. I negotiated the scooter forward and saw a motorcycle beside the road and the bodies of two women, their clothing on fire. There was another bike in the road that belonged to an ARVN soldier. I couldn't see him, but when I looked down where I had my boot on the ground to steady the scooter, I saw his boot with the lower part of one leg sticking up. The leg muscle was split and hung over the top of the boot. It was standing there, upright as though it belonged there.

We later determined the two women were VC and they had a satchel charge on the bike. They must have collided with the ARVN soldier causing the charge to go off, killing all three of them. If we had not stopped for gas, we might have been right there. Jim and I were shaken by the event. At that point, it brought home to me that this war was not going to have a successful conclusion and my doubts increased the longer I stayed. Nevertheless, I wasn't torn by my doubts and beliefs. I believed what I was doing had to be done, and should be done, to the best of my ability. It never crossed my mind to do anything less.

Therefore, that is how I came to view things. They say opinions are like assholes, everybody has one. Didn't know whether mine were right or wrong but I thought they were correct. I was eventually proven right, sadly, after many more lives were lost and much treasure squandered.

WHAT NOT TO DO

by Robin Bon-Jorn

I arrived in Vietnam in May 1967, for what was to be a one-year tour. However, my tour was not to last that long. My unit 1st Marine, 2nd Battalion, 7th Marines, Company G was stationed about five miles outside of Da Nang on the top of a small hill with a trench running around the bottom.

Our base consisted of six tents, each forty feet long, and a mess tent. The shower was outside on a wooden platform right next to the rice patties where women worked in the fields.

One of the first incidents happened the morning the guy in the bunk next to me stepped outside. Even though we had twenty-four hour armed lookouts keeping watch, he was struck by a mortar round which blew his arm off and riddled the tent with shrapnel. I never felt safe.

Many stories cannot be written or retold; for fear of repercussions from some of the "do-gooders" in our country.

My stay lasted only two and half months. I was a sergeant and squad leader, and every night I was out in the field on nighttime ambushes. We walked the trails, firing into the darkness and received hostile fire in return. On one occasion, another patrol called in to base and reported hearing shots fired (400 rounds in 15 seconds) and requested assistance, which resulted in our shooting at each other. This only happened to me once, but that's what they call friendly fire. We sent up a yellow flare, which stopped the shooting.

On my final mission, we had just pulled an all-nighter. I was anxious to get my men back to base so they could sleep, but we had to go help another unit. It was my first daytime mission and the sun was shining. One of the few times, I was not scared shitless.

At the outset, I needed to get the point man back to my squad leader position, the thirteenth in line, to show him on the map where I wanted him to go. Being the impatient person that I am, I decided to go forward to the point man. This was something a squad leader should not do. I should have stopped the squad and had the point man come back to me.

I got as far up between the point man and the second in line when I stepped on a landmine—one the point man missed. The explosion blew me five feet in the air and when I came back down on my back, I could see that my leg was mangled. Still fully conscious, I radioed for a medivac, and gave them our coordinates.

My men immediately formed a 360-degree circle around me. When a mine goes off it is normally followed by incoming fire, but none came. A chopper soon arrived but began to receive fire. If the fire is heavy, they have to cancel the mission.

At that point, I was scared, but they came in and got me. I was given morphine, taken to a field hospital for initial treatment and then transported to the Philippines. A short time later, I was headed stateside.

After a refueling stop in Alaska, I continued on to a hospital in Washington DC. Once stabilized, I was transported by bus to the Philadelphia Naval Hospital where I spent nine months in recovery.

During my stay there, I visited my previous point man, injured several weeks before me. He had lost his arm to a grenade. I found him in the psych ward lying in a bed arranged in a circle that reminded me of giant Ferris wheel. He was so out of touch with reality that he did not even recognize me. I saw a lot of people in far worse shape than me.

We were trained to break things and kill people. There was never any discussion as to why we were there. WE DID OUR JOB.

Sergeant Joseph Robin Bon-Jorn, USMC

TWO DEATHS, TWO LIVES

by Patrick McCrary

There are times when things happen and what took place is not what should have happened. Strange. Being young and inexperienced at life can leave a Marine vulnerable to the harshness of the reality and horror of combat. They are unable to prepare for them, no matter how good the training may be. The trick is to learn from the experience and not die. Even though in the throes of conflict, one dies a little each time.

Early morning hours in Vietnam was when most Marines preferred to do the "humping." That means hiking with "full gear" movements. If there was a cool part of the day, that was it. Most of the time, a low-lying mist or fog would be present, keeping the vegetation damp, green and lush. Everything was still and quiet. All seemed to be at peace, but that was an illusion—no rest for the weary in a war zone. You constantly had to change your position, hoping to keep the enemy off guard.

In Vietnam, enemy eyes were everywhere.

At daybreak, early in the spring of 1968, my platoon received orders to relocate. As the newest member of the platoon, I was given the point man duties and ordered to follow a series of trails that would take us to our new location. It was almost like walking next to one of the many lakes around my hometown of Clermont, Florida. Cool and misty, still and damp.

As I led our column, we came upon an intersection of several well-traveled trails, when out of nowhere an enemy soldier appeared. He was walking toward me with his rifle slung over his shoulder, looking down at the ground as he walked barefoot through the mucky, washed out area he had entered.

At first, I froze, startled by his sudden appearance, not much more than a shadow in the mist. I had my rifle at the ready, fully locked and loaded. I took aim at him and called out "Dung Lie" (halt). He was trying to get his rifle off his shoulder when I opened fire with my M-16. I squeezed off round after round, but he didn't go down. He was only 20 meters from me. I couldn't believe I wasn't hitting him.

I ceased fire, hoping he would raise his hands in surrender. He let out a low, mournful cry that sent a chill up my spine, and then he fell into the mud, mortally wounded. I raced to his position, fully expecting more of the enemy to be close behind. If there were any, they had retreated.

Standing over the enemy solider, I wanted to fire a final round into his head, to end his suffering. Instead, something touched me, deep in my soul that went beyond my "Kill or Be Killed" training mentality. Something beyond my pride of being a Marine and killing an enemy soldier. Perhaps—shame. I had hit him six times out of the eleven rounds I fired. His blood oozed from the wounds into the mud as our eyes met and I felt a connection with him, something deeper than pity. A feeling that I knew him, had met him somewhere before, then a feeling of dread consumed me. He would soon be dead.

He was perhaps ten years older than I, talking to me in Vietnamese, in a pitiful, crying whisper that I was unable to understand. I wanted to cry and hold him in my arms, to comfort him in his last few minutes on Earth, as I hoped someone would comfort me. He, like me, was some mother's son. Our two lives had crossed that morning for a reason I still do not fully understand. I silently watched his life slip away.

As I reflected on what was happening, it occurred to me there were two deaths this morning. The instant the enemy soldier died, my belief that we were helping the Vietnamese people also died.

I didn't like what had happened. I felt like throwing up. All I wanted was to be home, in my room, to lie in my bed and be able to live life as I choose. Probably not one bit different from that of the enemy soldier. Perhaps all he wanted was to grow his rice, feed his family, love his wife and children, and live life in peace.

Too many forces brought our two lives together that morning for me even to ask why. God will reveal that to me in due time. I prayed his family would survive the rest of that terrible war. As I had set his spirit free from his flesh, he had set me free from the innocence of my youth. Two deaths, two lives...no answers, only questions.

To the brave man I killed...I am sorry.

COUNT ME
AMONG THE LUCKY ONES

by John Macdonald

I received my draft notice in July 1969 requesting I report August 1969. With mixed emotions and apprehension, I decided to join the Army and signed up for three years instead of the two-year program for several reasons. I was still living at home with my mom. My older brother and sister were already married and moved away with their own families. The DEP, Delayed Enlistment Program, allowed me to stay at home three months longer to help my mom. Plus, I had to sell a car I couldn't afford while in the service. The DEP also gave me a higher rank and more pay when I went active duty December 5, 1969.

My first stop was Fort Jackson, South Carolina, for basic training and AIT (Advance Infantry Training). It was physically tough and demanding. The mental harassment by the drill sergeant was probably harder than the physical part. Looking back, I realize it was necessary to toughen us up.

Coach Perrin's high school football practices were harder physically, but basic training was all about having each other's back. Life was no longer just about winning a football game. The game now involved staying alive.

Throughout basic training, a lot of fear and apprehension grew among my comrades about where we were going from here.

Prior to enlisting, I worked at Winn Dixie so they assigned me to Food Services. After Basic Infantry Training, it was on to AIT, which was cook school for me. They asked if anyone had any experience in preparing and cooking food. I raised my hand and said, "I worked as a meat cutter." Before I knew it, I was training other trainee cooks to learn the different types of meats and how to cut them.

Twelve weeks later, I got my orders to Vietnam, relieved I had trained in the Food Service Area and would be part of a support group instead of serving on the front line. However, being the type of war

Vietnam was, front lines were questionable. There were base camps, major supply depots, and smaller posts. There were also Artillery Batteries in small bases all over South Vietnam. Alpha, Bravo, and Charlie were firebases and their job consisted of providing fire support in the field and bush for the Infantry Forces.

After receiving my deployment orders, I was required to do an extra week of RV or Republic of Vietnam training. During that week, I learned necessary maneuvers for helicopter landing and takeoff. At this point, the apprehension and fear I felt earlier became more intense. I realized, "Oh Shit, I am really going over there."

From Fort Jackson, South Carolina, I flew to Oakland, California, and spent a week with hundreds of other guys, all waiting to ship out. During our stay, we were housed in airplane hangars and slept on army cots. Until it came our turn to fly out, we played pool and cards, drank beer, slept, and watched TV.

The day I departed, the flight over the Pacific was very quiet. The eerie quietness pretty much reflected everyone's mood. We were young and proud to serve our country, trained to do what we were told, even if that meant some of us might not come home.

The unknown was unsettling.

My orders sent me to Firebase Nancy, the Battalion of the 39th Field Artillery/1st and 39th located about 30 miles south of the DMZ, near the small town of Dong Ha. Our supply depot in Quang Tri Province was about 20 miles west and the Pacific Coast and the Gulf of Tonkin was maybe 50 miles east. Three or four weeks before my arrival, the Viet Cong had overrun Firebase Nancy. The casualty rate was high and forty to fifty of us were new replacements. Not a good feeling.

We landed first in Long Bin near Cam Ranh Bay and were there for about five or six days. During that time, we were issued our weapons, gear, fatigues, etc. We then flew north to Dong Ha on an AC-130 Hercules, about a two-hour ride, sitting sideways in web seats, facing each other. At about 18,000 to 20,000 feet, there was a loud explosion. Within thirty seconds, it was so smoky we could barely see each other. The plane rocked, shook, and then made a quick nosedive. We started yelling and saying other expletives as well as, "This is it, we're gonna die."

A few seconds later, the plane leveled off and the co-pilot came back and tried to calm us down.

"No reason to be alarmed," he said. "The seal of the cargo door ramp blew out and caused the pressurized air in the cabin to rush out. Cold air mixed in with the warmer air in the aircraft and created the fog. The pilot had to dive the plane down to a lower altitude so we could breathe. Everything is fine now and we should be landing soon."

His explanation eased our fears but at first when everything started happening we thought for sure we had been shot down— so much for being new in-country.

The landing in Dong Ha was rough. The plane rolled down the runway swerving around rocket and mortar holes in the artificial metal landing strip. From there we went by truck to Firebase Nancy. That was in May 1970 and for the next couple of months everybody remained on edge.

A firebase is a circular compound equipped with heavy artillery guns, including self-propelled cannons. They sit on top of a tank chassis and are capable of firing shells several miles away to support the Infantry Forces in the bush or field.

After reinforcing the perimeter damaged in the earlier attack, things got back to normal. I was stationed there from May 1970 to April 1971. During that year, we built bigger foxholes outside our huts. The huts were plywood buildings with screens for windows and housed five or six people.

We had electricity when the generator worked, but it broke down a lot. Unfortunately, having gotten used to the loud hum, when it quit in the middle of the night, it was dead quiet.

Our mess hall was located in the center of the base in another plywood building. It contained a normal military kitchen and we cooked on field ranges that resembled large Coleman camping stoves that slid into metal cabinets.

We fed everybody three times a day and kept coffee and soup ready for shifts in the guard towers at night. Ten cooks, including the mess sergeant and me, worked in shifts so we could get some downtime. Once a week we would take turns riding shotgun to Quang Tri to pick up rations for our base.

I remember there was a one-lane bridge we had to cross. While trucks crossed from one direction, we had to wait and then we could cross. The bridge was located on the edge of a village and there were always a bunch of kids wanting candy bars, etc. If we sat there too long, people would try to steal stuff out of the back of our truck. Sometimes they were merely hungry kids but other times they were serious thieves. When we showed our weapons, they left us alone.

There were days like that and then others were quiet.

At night, sitting on top of our bunkers, we could see the flashes in the distance and knew the B-52s were bombing the Laos border (the Ho Chi Minh Trail). This helped keep the supply lines into Vietnam disrupted, making it harder for the VC to get supplies and reinforcements.

Besides cooking, I did a lot of carpentry. We built a large water tower frame to support a 1200-gallon water tank salvaged from a truck hit by a rocket-propelled grenade. Gravity forced running water from the tank to the mess hall where we fed 100 to 150 people every day.

Monsoon season made life miserable as it rained all the time, almost never stopping in the summer. During the rainy season, the military hired Vietnamese workers to do our laundry and they would dry our fatigues in the smokehouse used for fish. We had clean laundry but we all smelled like fish. Since everybody smelled the same, it didn't matter.

Our compound was located on high ground up from a river. High and low areas were cut into and dug out of the hills for safety. Occasionally, we were on the receiving end of a rocket or a mortar attack on the perimeter inside the concertina wire. Most times the damage was minor.

It was their way of harassing us.

One night we were firing tear gas down toward the river. The guard towers thought they had seen movement. Everyone was in our hooch, except me. I was sitting in the latrine, reading the comics. I was almost done when my eyes started burning a little. I finished up and stepped out only to see all my buddies standing outside wearing gas masks. The wind had shifted and blew the tear gas back in our direction. When they were told to put the mask on, I was twenty yards down the hill. Walking back, my friends wearing their masks said that I was protected in my own gas. I got teased about that for a while.

Thanksgiving and Christmas were okay. Our families sent care packages, usually our favorite goodies from home. Letters were always welcomed.

I'd say most of my year was uneventful except for a minor role in the Lam Son Operation in February 1971 aimed at cutting the Ho Chi Minh Trail in Laos and artillery support along with other units and firebases. If memory serves me right, we supported the Khe Sanh area.

When we became short timers, almost time to go home, one couldn't wait to leave. When we arrived in May of 1970, we were methodically herded around to our different destinations until we arrived at our final base. Funny thing though, going home was the opposite. Once I received my orders to go home, I had to turn in my weapon and find my own transportation from the Firebase Nancy to Da Nang.

I caught a ride on a military mail truck, and then boarded a small military transport. I think it was a C-123 twin-engine transport aircraft. I flew from Da Nang to Cam Ranh Bay and remained there a few days before flying to Tacoma, Washington, on a commercial jet liner.

Until the plane was in the air, one could hear a pin drop, and then everybody cheered. Prior to landing, we were instructed to walk in small groups once inside the airport, especially on the West Coast, so the protestors would leave us alone. After that, everything was pretty much back to normal and we either went home or to our next duty station.

In my case, I was stationed at Fort Riley, Kansas, for the next 16 months. One of the best things to come out of my time there was meeting the woman who became my wife. During that time, I also spent six weeks TDY in Germany participating in some maneuvers.

Jonlen and I married July 8, 1972 and moved to Florida September 1972. I went back to work at Winn Dixie for a year and a half, and then worked as a carpenter for nine years until I went to school to become a dental technician and retired in 2011. My wife and I are the proud parents of two sons, Jeff and Jason. In 2013, we moved back to Clermont. Home sweet home. My how it has changed from the days of my youth.

Specialist 5th Class/U.S. Army
John Macdonald
November 22, 2015

TOO CLOSE FOR COMFORT

by Joe Koester

I arrived in Vietnam in March 1969 assigned to MACV HQ as an I Corps analyst, replacing a fellow named Tom Fogarty. With only a week of overlap with Tom, one of the first orders of business was a trip up country to the Phu Bai Combat Base about 40 miles south of the DMZ. Tom and I, along with another analyst named Ron Hackley, caught an aircraft heading north. Upon arriving at the base, I was introduced to the Army Security Agency personnel and others whom I would be working with and supporting. We had a few beers that evening, and I was housed in the Bachelor Officer's Quarters that first night.

Early the next morning I heard loud explosions and an Army captain, clad only in his shorts and T-shirt, came running through yelling, "Incoming."

At first I didn't know who was coming in but as I fully awakened and heard more explosions, I figured out we were under attack and followed him out the door. Exiting the building, I saw an enormous orange flash to my right followed by another explosion and saw other soldiers running across the road to a bunker, yelling for me to follow. Then another explosion detonated, from what I later learned were Soviet 122 mm Katyusha Rockets.

Having never made it to the bunker, I found myself in a drainage ditch with the captain. Soon it was all over, with damage limited to some buildings. Tom exclaimed, "What am I doing here with only three days to go in-country?"

On another occasion, a few of us headed out of Saigon for a trip to a now-forgotten base out in III Corps. Dean, an Air Force lieutenant colonel, and Ken, an Army sergeant 1st class, accompanied me. We couldn't get a direct flight to our destination, so we hopped aboard a tiny helicopter with no doors that looked like an egg with a tail attached. It held only four passengers and, due to the curvature of the body, when I looked straight down, I could see the ground. The pilot took us to a clearing in the jungle and dropped us off assuring us another chopper would arrive soon to take us to our destination.

He left and it was as quiet as could be. We were in the middle of nowhere with a couple of side arms and M-16s. I was beginning to think that this wasn't going to turn out well. Soon a large Huey helicopter arrived and I quickly jumped aboard. Buckling myself into the seat, a colonel across from me asked, "And where are you headed, young man?"

When I told him, he informed me that they were not going there, but were on a tour of the Fire Support Bases. I knew what they were and did not want to go there. The pilot called and found that our helicopter would soon be arriving. I got out and they took off.

What felt like an eternity later, another chopper landed. The pilot said that he could not take us to where we were going, but he would get us out of there.

When we landed beside a metal covered runway, I got out and started charging across the runway toward the buildings on the far side. Then I heard one of my buddies shouting a warning. I was in the middle of the runway and a twin-engine aircraft was landing.

Once the other plane landed, we scurried across and found we were in Lai Khe, which had the dubious distinction of being "the most rocketed city in South Vietnam," or so the sign on the operations building read. It turned out that Lai Khe was also the base of a helicopter gunship battalion. We asked about transportation back to Saigon. Having given up on wherever we were originally going, we were told they weren't running a taxi business.

We soon met the unit commander, an Army major, and I discovered it was very handy to have a lieutenant colonel along, even if he was Air Force. Rank has its privileges. The major agreed to have one of his choppers take us back to Saigon, and told the pilot to give us a "special ride," and that he did. He flew low and fast. The best helicopter ride I ever had, and I got some great pictures from my perch beside the door gunner.

Another memorable trip was up to I Corps on a C-130 transport. We landed at Da Nang and then headed for Phu Bai. When we landed, the cargo master had the ramp down. The aircraft never quite stopped, yet he signaled for us to get out. I should have realized that this was not a normal landing for Phu Bai. As usual, I was the first to jump out and headed for the terminal when I saw a sign that said "Welcome to Dong Ha." Not wanting to spend the night or longer, I raced back for the aircraft and managed to leap aboard. We landed at Phu Bai a short time later and went about our business.

In our MACV office, we generated a lot of classified reports, papers, maps, etc. that had to be disposed of from time to time. This meant gathering up all the burn bags and hauling them over to another facility where someone placed them in an incinerator. This was a messy job usually left to the few enlisted personnel in our office, but they had to be accompanied by an officer or civilian. I volunteered and a couple of us drove a van loaded with burn bags over to the incinerator.

As a reward for this "extra duty," they gave us a day off; one day of R&R to Vung Tau on the Pacific Coast. We flew down on a Central Intelligence Agency (Air America) C46 and enjoyed a day on the beach. Some young ladies were offering their services. One attractive gal approached me. I declined her offer but referred her to an Army sergeant named George and off they went.

My friend Ken, an Army sergeant 1st class, and another guy went for a swim with me in the ocean. We were enjoying the water when the lifeguard started blowing his whistle and frantically gestured for everyone to get out of the water. We started in when Ken gave out a yell and ran ahead. When he hit the beach, he put down bloody footprints. He had been bitten by a poisonous sea snake. The medics gave him a couple of shots and put him on a chopper to the military hospital at Bien Hoa.

Ken came back a few days later, the side of his foot was black and he limped around some. We were told that the Vietnamese usually died from these bites, as they do not get the shots and airlifted to a hospital.

I ended up with severe sun poisoning on both feet and the medic said to spread Preparation H on the tops of both feet (worked great) and to wear shower clogs with my uniform. That got some curious looks from the officers I encountered. And George, well...he came down with a bad case of venereal disease.

On the return from one of my last trips to Phu Bai, I started to feel sick as we were boarding the twin-engine intelligence gathering aircraft. Minutes into the trip, I felt so bad I ended up lying on the floor of this small eight or ten passenger aircraft. Burning up with fever, I soon became delirious and was slurring my words.

The pilot radioed for an ambulance to meet us when we landed at Tan Son Nhut where I was taken to the 3rd Field Hospital. By then I had a temperature of 106 and the trots. They worked on me, stopped the diarrhea and then they wanted a stool sample. That is when this orderly came around with an Electrolux vacuum cleaner wand and abused me.

At first, the medical staff thought I had malaria and was slated to be air evacuated to Japan. Then they called it FUO (Fever of Unknown Origin). When they weren't looking, I retrieved my uniform and walked out. Since I was never accounted for, I may still be listed among the missing.

MILITARY TACTICS

(The Ambush)

by Patrick McCrary

Military tactics are something civilians might scratch their heads and wonder about, but a combat Marine knows they are designed and used for a variety of reasons, depending on the required results. For example, the tactics might be to cause confusion, to disperse troops, or to secure and search dense and open areas. Without a doubt, inflicting terror is the most effective tactic. When used and executed correctly, an ambush can terrorize and demoralize an entire unit.

During the Vietnam War, the Viet Cong were also familiar with the power of the ambush. In a combat situation, as night approached, it was "most advisable" to set up defensive positions, plan the night watch rotations and get your perimeter as secure as possible.

On August 4, 1968, A Company, First Battalion, Fifth Marines (1/5) Regiment conducted a methodical seek-and-destroy mission in the An Hoa basin of South Vietnam. I was the new guy in the platoon—a rifleman, trained to follow orders and do Marine stuff. I liked doin' Marine stuff.

We had been humping all day, doing online sweeps, village searches, ambushes and patrols, over and over, trying to secure as large an area as possible. It was late in the afternoon when I spotted what I thought was a lone VC in the tree line just ahead of us, at about 200 meters. I pointed out to the rest of my platoon where I had seen the enemy as I opened fire with my M-16.

The VC took cover behind a tree.

Everyone "zeroed-in" on him. Can you imagine the firepower of a platoon of Marines? We tore that area apart. Then the lieutenant ordered us to cease fire and the second squad to get on line and sweep the tree line to confirm a body count, as we were sure we would have a kill.

When we crossed the shrub line between

the tree line and us, we saw the mounds, scores of them. We had entered a Vietnamese graveyard. The Vietnamese bury their dead in a sitting, fetal position so that the graves are mounds, circular in design; their size varies depending on the size of the corpse.

The sun was setting in the west as we entered into the shadows of the tree line. Racing to the location and trying to stay spread out, we were only 30 meters from our objective, working our way through the graves, when the world split open and the Devil himself jumped out. Explosions, machine gun fire, rifle fire, incoming gunfire, white tracers hitting the ground in front of my face, the screams of my comrades...all in an instant.

The machine gun firing at me was only 15 meters away. I could smell the gunpowder from his muzzle blast.

We had walked right into them. They baited us with one lone body just off their flank and drew us in.

I was pinned down 15 meters from a machine gun with night approaching. *Oh God, what is that moaning?* It was Sonny, the Marine on my right, between the machine gun and me. I'd somehow fallen to the ground behind a small grave. Sonny was in a depression between two graves, almost a swale in the graveyard.

He was five meters from the machine gun when they sprung the ambush. Now he was just below their line of fire. We established communications and I discovered he was unable to move. I found out later, he had been hit nine times. From my limited cover I was able to return gunfire and keep the machine guns quiet for short periods. I saw and fired at the enemy as they tried to get closer to our "make-do" cover. Sonny and I, plus another Marine, killed instantly, were in the crossfire of A Company 1/5 and the enemy. We were seeing white (enemy) and red (friendly) tracers crossing and coming very close to us.

You haven't lived until you've almost died. To see, feel, and hear machine gun bullets stitch the ground next to you and experience the terror it brings, qualifies for both. Bullets moved so fast it is truly hard to describe their impact on something firm. Suddenly, it seemed dark, I couldn't see. I had lost my night vision with the first muzzle flashes.

Mercifully, Sonny was not in extreme pain. He sought reassurance from me about our predicament.

I assured him he was stuck with me and not to worry, I could defend our position. Before the sun fully set I located a large grave five meters behind us. It would help shield us from the incoming fire our platoon was directing at the VC. I tried several times to get to Sonny's position but the automatic weapons fire prevented me from advancing across the open area between us. I moved to the larger grave so I would be able to protect our position. Every few minutes I engaged the enemy in a firefight and took shots at their movements to keep them off us.

Night falling around us, it became apparent Sonny was losing strength. I figured he was dying. As he gained and lost consciousness, we both prayed and talked of home.

I also used the time to reload my expended clips, 18 rounds per clip, and I carried 12 fully loaded clips, with enough spare rounds to reload six more. I had 18 clips with 18 rounds each. Plenty of ammo in most firefights, but for this one it wasn't. The area was alive with the enemy.

I called out to the rest of the platoon at the top of my voice, "Sonny and I are still alive. We need help." I didn't understand until later that all the Marines in A 1/5 had received orders to stay back. The VC had set one trap, another was sure to follow.

During the night, the rest of the platoon ceased fire because of the uncertainty of our position. I continued expending my ammo. The VC movements were getting closer every time the flares burned out. By this time, the C.O. had called in night flares to try to locate us and in case, Sonny and I could use the light. I clenched my jaws. *Thank you, lieutenant, we are lying in the middle of an open graveyard and you're lightin' the place up like a Friday night high school football game. God bless you, sir.*

The VC and I traded rifle fire. They finally got lucky and three rounds struck me. One burrowed under my flak jacket, taking a chunk of flesh from my shoulder, one pierced my E-tool and the other penetrated my pack. By midnight, I had used both grenades and all but seven rounds of ammo. I hadn't been able to get Sonny to respond to me for over an hour. *Why doesn't he respond? Oh God, has he died?*

By this time, I decided it best for me to leave my two fallen comrades and make my way back to the rest of the Company. I was almost out of ammo and the VC was closing in with every minute that passed. They were virtually in our position now.

I dropped my pack and flak jacket and began to low crawl through the graveyard. When I came across my other fallen Marine brother, I took his rifle and ammo, and then continued. After crawling through the graveyard and penetrating the brush line, I looked in the direction from which we had originally come. There, in all their glory, was A 1/5, the most wonderful sight in the world. I thought of a row of ducks as their heads silhouetted against the flares in the background. Having no password I was forced to call out to my comrades not to be mistaken as the enemy. I was safe.

As morning approached, we moved at the first crack of light to the graveyard to find Sonny miraculously clinging to life. He was able to look me in the eye and said, "Mac, you saved my life last night."

The pride I felt was beyond anything that had ever happened to me. Not because I had survived the terror, not because he thought I saved his life, but because I was a combat Marine. We did not retreat. We stayed with our fallen brothers to the end.

That night, Sonny proved to me there are no Ex-Marines—"Once a Marine, always a Marine." The courage and determination, shown by Sonny, continues to paint the everlasting image of what the title "United States Marine" really stands for. We are always as one.

Marines don't leave Marines on the battlefield. *Semper Fi* (Always Faithful) is our motto. Being the "First to Fight" is our mission. *Esprit de Corps* (The Spirit of the Corps) is a feeling that only Marines can know. God Bless Sonny. God Bless the Corps. God Bless America.

THE SOLDIER I BECAME

by Kent Swanson

My father was a patriot. His love for his family, God, and country inspired me to get more out of my life than anyone else ever would. He put his life on the line for what he believed in when he was a young man, by fighting for our way of life in the Battle of the Bulge in World War II. He manned a 20 mm cannon and lost much of his hearing but not his life as he watched many of his friends die around him. When he returned, he probably felt that same sense of relief and joy to be safely back home that I and most of my military brothers experienced returning from the Vietnam conflict.

When I now see the sense of entitlement

that many of our young people seem to have today, I have to ask myself "what motivates them to be like that?"

My dad helped me to love people and to give back despite the "takers" around me. Wanting to be more than I was when I graduated from Clermont High in 1970, with my parents' encouragement, I went off to college in Illinois. I studied physics and had a deferment from the draft. But after my second year in college, my high school sweetheart's father committed suicide and her life was turned upside down. My love for her, prompted me to marry her and join the Air Force. With the love of my life by my side, we chose my dad as best man.

The Vietnam War was under way when I joined the military, but I never thought that I would be sent there. For three of my four years, I was an aircraft maintenance crew chief on C-130 Hercules cargo planes. I was placed on worldwide mobility status, which required me to support many different missions around the world and be ready to leave within an hour, 24 hours a day.

During that time, I traveled all over Europe and Asia. With my name on the side of the plane and part of the flight crew, I flew *my* plane around the world, involved in everything from paratrooper drops, to carrying nuclear bombs. I traveled to places that few people have been, and cannot talk about it.

Late in my second year of military enlistment, I trained on OV-10 Bronco aircraft. With special high tech optic systems, they were the latest forward air controllers over Vietnam. These were the hottest little "sports cars" of the sky, powered by turbine engines, sported ejection seats, armor, laser designators, four machine guns, and could carry multiple weapons under its wings, such as white phosphorus rockets. Their missions ranged from supporting jungle rescue by the "jolly green" helicopters under fire to directing F-4 supersonic precision bombings of the Ho Chi Minh trail, using napalm or other bombs.

On the airbase in the jungle, we frequently contended with the threat of mortar attacks from enemies outside of the perimeter fence. Our M-16 rifles were nearby all the time, but our aircraft were generally the targets of attacks. Other than mortar explosions, our biggest fear was from cobras and "one stepper" snakes (kraits) that hid under the revetment panels making up the airplane parking areas. Our planes were kept separated from each other in case one was struck by a mortar. That way, maybe only one plane would be destroyed along with the people nearby.

Like everyone who fought in this jungle conflict, the war took some of my friends.

Everyone in a war loses something.

Returning from Vietnam, I was happy to have survived, but damaged in ways that can't be seen. I have nightmares every night and most of the time I wake to say, "It's just another dream." I have lost some hearing due to turbine engine noise and gunfire. In addition, I hear ringing in my ears all the time. Even now, I am always aware of my surroundings and on edge to protect myself. I guess I'll always be the soldier I was made to be. Assigned back to the USA, I finished the remainder of my military time traveling the world again in my C-130 aircraft.

Another casualty of war for me was coming home to an empty house. My time away at war was too much for my wife. We later reconciled and created a family with two sons.

After my military service, I moved back to Florida and got my degree in physics. I worked for Martin Marietta several years designing many weapons systems for the government. The list includes "nap of the earth" maneuvering of aircraft, laser designating aircraft systems, ground control radar for missile weapons, and a radar system mounted above the rotor blades of the Apache helicopter, creating the Longbow Apache. Many systems are still fielded by the military to this day.

I also contributed designs to the Pershing missile system, and sometimes joke that things around me are not rocket science, and, as a rocket scientist, I should know. Like my dad, I became a patriot and am glad that I have been able to contribute to our freedom. I most appreciate the freedoms that we take for granted because of the many sacrifices made by our military personnel. Some sacrifices more horrible than others.

My experience in Vietnam would not be complete without sharing a story about the cuisine. The most popular snack for the locals in Southeast Asia was a bug, Maeng Da. We called them rice bugs. They resembled the Florida water bug or maybe a giant cockroach with crab claws. Their stomachs were filled with rice from the rice fields they fed on.

I once saw a local who worked in our chow hall catch one that flew in through the front door. He bit the head off and sucked the guts out right in front of us. Obviously, an acquired taste. I never tried them.

A lizard I saw there also deserves mention. If you were out at night and went to the latrine, you might be surprised by the sound of the "fuck you" lizard. It is so named by us because it sounds exactly like someone saying, "fuck you."

So does my story have a happy ending?

I survived the Vietnam War. My dad and the love of my life have since died. Thanks to John Hotaling and the CHS Alumni Newsletter, I reconnected with a good friend from my high school class who was a widow. She understands the haunting nightmares of the Vietnam War, having been married to a Vietnam soldier for many years. We both have a life to live and have gained comfort from sharing our past as we discover new adventures. Yes, there is a happy ending.

THE UNDOCUMENTED CASUALTIES OF THE VIETNAM WAR

by Ruth Stewart Robinson-Swanson

When I went to a Veterans Service Office to apply for widow's benefits I was told, "You aren't the veteran and never served in war." Questioning what the officer was telling me. I replied, "My husband was in Vietnam for two years fighting that war. I lived with him thirty-seven years after he came home and I can tell you, I lived that war every day. Don't tell me that I didn't serve in a war. I took care of him, helped to keep him safe, cried when he cried and became angry at all the reasons he was angry about." This is my husband's story from a wife's perspective.

I graduated from Clermont High School in 1970—the same year my future husband was in the midst of his experience in Vietnam. Bill served in the Army from 1969-1971. His paperwork listed him as being in the infantry but his stories suggested some of his assignments were more like being in Special Forces.

When I met him in 1975, he was a musician in a band in Las Vegas, Nevada. Charming and talented, Bill was a good man, kind and generous, a good provider, and we raised a blended family of mine, his, ours, and two foster children. In spite of his good qualities, he had problems with alcohol, drugs, nightmares, and flashbacks that intensified as he got older. The love of my life died in 2011 from complications of PTSD, COPD, and alcoholism. He had been on VA disability for ten years and suffered from not only nightmares, but also blackouts. He slept with his eyes open until the day he died.

Our children remember well the obsession their father had with survival. Bill started gathering supplies back in the 80s after we moved to Florida. We had purchased seven acres of land to build a home south of Clermont. He loved the swamp and would dress up in his fatigues and gear, hike through them, clearing areas to build trails and put up lean-to structures for shelter. Our two sons who were home at the time would go with him. He treated them like his soldiers. They called him Sarge. They practiced maneuvers day and night. He taught them skills that would help them survive if war came to the United States, but he didn't encourage them to join the military. Their father didn't teach them about life in the business world, nor did he emphasize them getting a college education or learning a trade.

Bill didn't trust the government and didn't want to ask for help from the Veterans Administration. He was afraid someone was watching him and they knew all the things he had done in Vietnam. He was scared and guarded, even when he went to bed at night, sleeping with one eye open and at times, both. When he was around other people, he would not let anyone know he felt vulnerable. He appeared strong and ready to defend at all times.

Two events surfaced in his discussions with the family after Bill finally admitted he had a problem and agreed to seek professional assistance. Both events broke our hearts hearing his pain.

During his first tour in Vietnam, a group

of fellow soldiers raped my husband the night before he was to go on leave to be married to his first wife in 1969. He was embarrassed and ashamed. Dealing with the feelings of pain and helplessness, he didn't report the rape. If he had, they would have started an investigation and probably kept him there. Afraid they would do it again if he told, Bill ignored his feelings, stuffed the anger down, and finally got to the place of "don't mean nothing." An expression I heard others say during counseling meetings later at the VA.

Bill withdrew and became a loner. He was used for missions but was forbidden to discuss them. Some of his lead officers accused him of having a bad attitude, but he just didn't care. He had no friends, was afraid to get close to people and didn't trust anyone. He once told his doctor that he was having a hard time even trusting his immediate family. I was his third wife and he had been out of the Army for four years when we married.

The other event he told us about was during his second tour. He remembered an ambush outside the area of LZ Ellen that happened during the day. About ten soldiers from the platoon were out on patrol. They stopped and split off to patrol a trail they found. Somewhere about 200 meters farther, they were ambushed.

Everyone dropped and started firing back. It lasted only a minute or two. Then there was a lull, like the eye of a storm, followed by more firepower from the enemy again, this time using B40 rockets. Two or three guys had one of the rockets explode in a tree right above them. The platoon returned fire.

Bill told us he was on the ground under a log that swayed up a little. He fit under the log and could look under and fire his shots up and above instead of rising and firing over the log. Finally, he heard someone shout, "Cease fire." Shots ceased. Then he heard the rest of the platoon going around to help the wounded, the lieutenant being among them.

Bill got up to check for dead North Vietnamese Army (NVA). As he walked up and around from the position where he'd been firing from, he realized he'd been bitten by a spider.

He went to the Quan Loi Hospital to be checked. They told him he could wait it out or start taking the shots in his stomach as the treatment called for. Bill decided to wait it out and returned to the field. When he didn't hear anything more about the lieutenant, he wondered if the lieutenant had died from the B40 rockets, enemy fire, or shots fired by him and the guy next to him from their position under the log.

He never knew the real truth and it haunted him until he died.

Many people have been affected by wars: the enlisted soldiers, their spouses and children waiting at home, their parents, siblings, aunts, uncles, and best friends from high school. Pain from memories can haunt and torture. Some veterans have been disabled physically, probably more mentally, both a greater sacrifice than imagined possible. Forgiveness and love can assist in the healing, but the greatest healing comes from God. May my late husband now rest in peace.

THE TWO-LEGGED DOG

by Patrick McCrary

It seems life is nothing more than a series of joy and difficulties, peaks and valleys, good and bad, yin and yang. In combat situation—all that changes. There is no good, only bad, no ups only downs. Only if you have been there can you know. I have been there and I can say that there is an exception to every rule.

While on patrol in the An Hoa region of Vietnam, we were to move into an area that had been sprayed with Agent Orange. In the process, our platoon came across a village that was supposed to have been blown off the map with air strikes by F4 Phantoms, the most awesome aircraft in the sky. A terrible weapon of war. It was obvious that a great catastrophe had occurred here. However, the people were friendly and greeted us with warm smiles, fresh water and open arms.

I was amazed at their ability to smile, much less welcome strangers and gun totin' ones at that.

As we secured the village and made sweeps of the area, it became obvious we were in a special place. All the hooches were beaten up. All the people were beaten up. But they smiled and carried on with their lives.

My squad was given C.P. security, which meant we guarded the Command Post. This allowed us to move more freely among the locales. We Marines were worn out. It was mid-October, hot and humid. It rained every day and most nights. We frowned, but they smiled—all of them. It was nice to be among natives who accepted us.

A few hours after we arrived, one of my fire team leaders came to me and said, "Mac, you gotta see this."

My first reaction was "Don't fuck with me man, what's up?"

To which he replied, "I'm not gonna tell ya. You gotta' see this."

The urgency and surprise in his voice piqued my curiosity. "All right, all right," I said. "Let's go."

Moving through the village, I could see the locals smiling at us.

When we entered an open area on the outskirts of the village, a group of kids were playing with a dog—one with two legs.

Now mind you, he had four legs but was walking, running and playing with the village kids up on his two front legs. The dog had been hit by a piece of shrapnel in the lower spine, just in front of his hips. The wound had healed, but his rear legs had reverted to a shrimp-like tail tucked into his belly area.

I could not believe what I was seeing. A smile crept across my face as I watched this dog, perfectly balanced on his two front legs, walking and, yes, running in short bursts. *My God, what sort of animal could live through such despair, such pain, such utter hopelessness?*

A mangy dog with a heart the size of Texas.

As I reflected on what I was witnessing, a tear traced down my cheek. Just then, an old lady, with teeth black from chewing the betel nut root, gently took my hand. She looked me in the eyes and shook her head. Then she smiled and pointed to the dog.

Somehow I knew what she was saying. If that dog could be satisfied with his life, then so should I. In that moment, I was reborn.

The devastation that had been inflicted on those people was beyond description. In their desperation, the villagers drew strength and a will to live from the animal's example.

I think that dog was one of God's angels, put there for the villagers.

The example shown by a mangy dog provided them with hope for a better day, that they too could survive and see this war to its conclusion.

Life would get better. Self-pity could serve no useful purpose.

We left the village a few hours after our encounter with the dog, never to return as we sometimes did in Vietnam. I never saw him again, but I will never forget the spirit and the will to live of that two-legged dog. All of us in the 2nd Platoon A Company 1/5 were somehow better people for having been in the presence of such a wondrous living example of the word *spirit*. What an animal.

MY VIETNAM EXPERIENCE

by Paul "Corky" Bruno

After high school, I went to work at Konsler Steel, Inc. in Clermont. Because of my prior experience drawing house plans for my father, I soon moved to the engineering department. I was working my way through college when I dropped out one semester to get married. And guess what? Dear ol' Uncle Sam sent me my draft notice. Instead of waiting to be drafted, I joined the Navy. Ten months after our wedding I shipped off to boot camp. I endured fourteen weeks of torment and another eighteen weeks of specialized training before being assigned to duty onboard the USS Stribling DD-867, a Navy destroyer.

The Stribling was small and met the criteria of being called a ship by a couple of feet. Maximum crew number was 300, but we usually ran with less than 200. For the next six weeks, we performed training exercises in the Caribbean, in preparation for a tour to Vietnam.

February 1969 we set sail for Vietnam. Being a hometown boy, I got homesick. Worse than being in boot camp. Our first stop was Panama Canal, then on to San Diego, California.

We stayed three days in San Diego to supply the ship. Believe it or not—it was snowing. During this stay, our ship was outfitted with 50 caliber machine guns, anti-aircraft guns, and depth charges. They also loaded our ASROCs (anti-submarine rockets) and about 3,000 five inch 38 caliber rounds for our big gun. Along with the armaments, we stocked tons of food, water, fuel oil, and other supplies. Anything that could be loaded by hand was. Then we set sail again, headed for Hawaii for a three-day stay.

Along the route, we practiced shooting at targets trailed behind planes and behind our sister ship. Since most of our crew were novices, we almost sank our sister ship. One time, when practicing with the ASROCs, one was shot off the wrong side of the ship. Heads rolled for that mistake.

Hawaii was a good stop. By this time, I was already a 3rd class petty officer and had liberty all three days. I took a day tour of Honolulu, and then spent the rest of the time on Waikiki Beach.

Next stop was Midway, then on to Okinawa. I had liberty at Midway, but not at Okinawa. Still, I had fun on deck watching the goony birds and soon came to understand how they got their name. The water clear and blue, I would drop shiny bolts over the side and watch them sink over a hundred feet down with the birds diving in pursuit.

At night, I sat on the deck and watched the sparkle of lights in the water from some sort of crustaceans that glowed. The flying fish, some two feet long, would fly hundreds of yards a mere few feet above the water. Porpoises swam in our bow wake for miles. All these things fascinated me. However, since I was in the Navy, work beckoned me.

Our ship, built during World War II, was in need of much repair. While underway, deck hands chipped and painted the exterior of the ship, while I helped lag steam lines, chip and paint bilges, and other maintenance jobs to make the engine rooms bearable. As a machinist mate, I was assigned to the forward engine room. When we left home, the room temperature was near 120 degrees, but after all the lagging and repairs the temperature dropped to less than 100 degrees.

It took a while to get used to living aboard ship, especially the heads and bunking area. The heads consisted of ten toilets, no dividers or doors. Five toilets to a side facing each other. When all were being used, your shoulders touched and you would bump heads with the guy in front if you bent over. The berthing area was not much better. Where I slept was twenty-seven feet by thirty-six feet and berthed eighty men. The bunks were stacked three high with about eighteen inches between them and no more than twenty inches between rows.

Many nights we would have to strap ourselves in our bunks to keep from falling out when the ship rolled. Sometimes during storms, our ship would take on so much water that there would be six to seven inches in our berthing compartment. As the ship rolled from side to side, the water would collect on the lower side of the roll and engulf the bunks there. We then had to take turns using the midship bunks.

Eating was a challenge too. The plates we used were high-sided metal trays with four compartments. Sailing in rough seas, the green peas would roll up the sides and off your plate. We learned to hold the edge of the plate with one hand and tilt it with the rolling ship to keep it level. Many of my crewmates would get so seasick they would leave their plates and vacate the mess hall.

I never got seasick so I gladly finished their food.

The USS Stribling had a small hangar and a small flight deck to accommodate a drone. Our ship didn't have a drone, so we used this area for recreation. Each Sunday those who played instruments gathered there and we set up tables and had a barbecue. The time we left Mayport, Florida, and arrived at Yokosuka, Japan, took a month. Lights, music, and card games went on most every night.

Along with our sister ship we steamed toward Vietnam. After two weeks in the war zone, we relieved our sister ship for two, then we served another two weeks. Our captain always made sure we were in the war zone for payday. That way, our pay and any personal supplies we bought were tax-free. Payday was also a time we received more immunizations to go along with the sixty-seven we received in boot camp. It was a sweet and sour time.

Each time we entered the war zone we did something different. One of our duties was plane guarding for carriers operating on the "Yankee Station" in the Gulf of

Tonkin. We would steam behind aircraft carriers in case a plane missed the landing deck and crashed into the ocean. Then we would rescue the pilot and sit guard over the sunken plane until a salvage ship arrived.

Another time, we drew close to shore to support the Army and Marine ground troops. The USS Stribling drew only fourteen feet of water when loaded, so we could get really close to the shore. So close in fact, we could almost make out the faces of the people on shore. When we were that close, our deck hands also called "deck apes" would throw hand grenades over the side of the ship at night to discourage the Vietcong from swimming out and boarding our ship unnoticed.

At night, we fired magnesium flare rounds miles into the air to light up the beach and mountainside. Each time the gun fired, lightbulbs would explode, dust would fall down from overhead, and the whole ship would shake. Try sleeping through that.

During the daylight hours, we fired our big gun over the mountains to hit targets whose coordinates were radioed to us by helicopters. We blew up rice dumps, Vietcong tunnels, train trestles, and enemy convoys, among other things. On the beachside of the mountain, we sank sampans known to have the Vietcong onboard. Our total confirmed kills were 265.

We were informed daily over the intercom of our status.

I remember one day, a small two-man fishing boat passing between our ship and the shore capsized due to the shockwave produced by our 5"-38 guns. The men in the boat were warned to clear the area but had refused.

Our dress code included bulletproof vests and steel helmets whenever we were in sight of land and on deck. Let nobody kid you, those helmets and vests are heavy. After an hour or so wearing them, I would go inboard just to take them off.

Many events were memorable and exciting while we were in the war zone. Events like replenishing riverboats that came out to us for supplies. The stories these sailors told of their river conflicts were riveting. Then there was sitting on deck at night, watching the 2,000 pound shells fly overhead, shot from the 16-inch guns of the USS New Jersey battleship sitting forty miles off shore. Other times, we worked our butts off making enough steam to keep in sight of the aircraft carrier we were plane guarding.

The carrier steamed at 40 knots in a five-mile square while we moved at 31 knots in a circle inside that square, keeping the carrier in sight. Not as bad as it sounds. The fast speed allowed more air to be gathered by the air scoops and cool the engine room about twenty degrees.

One of the worst times in the war zone happened during the USS Pueblo incident. We had been on line for our two weeks and about to be relieved by our sister ship when, instead of relieving us, she was sent to North Korea. They were there for the entire two weeks of their war zone time. We then had to proceed with our regular two weeks on line that made our total time six weeks straight.

During that time, there were about four weeks I didn't even venture outside. The reason for this was being at combat stations, four hours on and four hours off. During my shifts, I would stand watch, unless it fell between the hours of 0800 and 1600 hours. This eight-hour span was taken up with good ole hard work. During the four hours of free time, I crammed in toilet time, took a shower, ate something and, oh yeah, got some sleep. Does the word "zombie" come to mind?

Food during this six-week period was another story. Not being able to replenish our supplies, fresh food soon vanished. We had to drink powdered milk and eat powdered potatoes made with powdered milk. Powdered eggs were on our breakfast menu and used for anything needing eggs. Fresh meat and loaf bread became a memory. Other things that happened during this time didn't mean too much. Things like fistfights, card playing, and stealing food were common events.

Missing my wife is what bothered me the most during the entire tour. Judy and I corresponded by sending cassette tapes to each other. I also took about ten hours of super eight movies and sent them home. Every port we entered, I called Judy and we would talk a long time. Those phone calls cost my wife almost all of her pay. I'm glad she thought I was worth it.

Although my Vietnam experience had some good and some bad, I did get to see many places. After steaming to and from the war zone, we had five to eight days to stay in each port visited. We visited ports like Okinawa, Nagasaki, and Yokosuka in Japan. In the Philippines, we ported at Olongapo (Subic Bay) two times. That was a wild place. We docked at Kaohsiung when visiting Taiwan. Hong Kong was a fun and a fascinating place to visit.

In each of these ports, I was able to tour a lot of the surrounding countryside. I traveled by train, bus, cab, and one time by bicycle, but no matter which way, I had fun. When our tour of duty in Vietnam ended, we set sail for home.

Our journey back to the States was not without incident. Sleeping on Waikiki Beach in Hawaii, I was rolled by three teenagers. After an hour chase and a short confrontation, I got back all my valuables. Between Hawaii and San Diego, we sailed through a hurricane. The rolling of the ship was so bad that we could walk on the walls easier than on deck. Our ship lost all power and we were dead in the water. During this time, an automated cargo ship sailed past within 50 feet of our bow. A little too close for comfort. However, we survived and arrived safely in San Diego. From San Diego, we went to Acapulco, Mexico, for three days and then Panama City for a day before returning to Mayport, FL.

For the first time in nine months, I was able to hug and kiss my wife. After a thirty-day leave, I bought an eighteen-foot travel trailer and moved it to a campground just off base in Mayport. Judy and I lived there for the next eight months. During this time, she became pregnant with our first child. I was soon to be a dad!

While in West Pac (Western Pacific), I injured my neck. The injury steadily worsened and led to my early release. Judy and I had already bought a home in Clermont, Florida, before our wedding so we moved back into it. I returned to my former job with Konsler Steel in Clermont, but was unable to work full-time for over a year because of the neck injury. I still have therapy from time to time, even forty-six years later.

Let me tell you, life is good. God brought me through it all.

WHY THAT CAN'T BE

by Joe Koester

Despite the conditions of working in stressful surroundings, guys will find the time to have fun. One evening, I was working the I Corps desk in our detachment at Military Assistance Command Vietnam Headquarters (MACV HQ) and decided to have a little fun with Jack Haynie, my counterpart working the day shift.

Jack had been dating a Vietnamese woman named Phoung who worked the desk at my Bachelor Officer's Quarters (BOQ) in Cholon (Saigon's Chinese District.) For the life of me, I couldn't figure how he got her to go out with him. Jack was an average looking guy, small stature, and this gal was really beautiful.

Jim Padgett, Jack's roommate, and I were working the night shift when we came up with the idea to pull a fast one on Jack. Many of us had telephones in our individual rooms so we could be called to work during a crisis. Jack had such a phone.

Using my best fractured French Vietnamese English I called Monsour Jacque and introduced myself as Nguyen, Miss Phoung's brother. Jack seemed surprised and happy to hear from him, and all bubbly until I said, "Mmm, Miss Phoung she hab baby."

To which Jack exclaimed, "Why that can't be."

I concluded the conversation with "I will kill yough," and hung up.

Jim and I laughed, quite pleased with ourselves until we realized that Jack was alone back in the BOQ with an M-16 and several magazines of ammunition. I mentioned to Jim that I was glad I didn't have to go back to that BOQ.

We examined our options and worried that a jittery Jack might shoot someone, I called back, identified myself and said, "Why that can't be."

He called me several well deserved names and that was the end of that, or sorta.

Later on, and for many subsequent years, I would run into Jack occasionally in the halls back at Headquarters and always greeted him with, "Why that can't be."

He threatened to get even with me but never did, and we all remembered the incident—a little humor in a serious and dark era.

Jack pulled another tour in Vietnam, up country, with the Marines at Da Nang. I was newly married and content to stay back in the Baltimore—Washington area. Jack never lived to enjoy retirement. He retired in December 1996 while in a hospital and died the next month.

He was a good man.

GROWING UP IN THE NAVY

by Michael McCrary

In 1965, a week after my seventeenth birthday, I dropped out of school and enlisted in the U.S. Navy for a four-year tour of duty. I went to boot camp at the Naval Training Center in Great Lakes, Illinois. Three months later, I was assigned to the CNIC Field Naval Air Station in Jacksonville, Florida where Navy pilots practiced landing and taking off. I spent thirteen months there, serving as part of a crash crew. If a plane crashed, it was our job to save the pilots and put out the fires. Two or three planes went down while I was stationed there.

During one rescue, the crash crew almost ran over the pilot. He was taking off and had a flame out, a sudden stop of the jet's engine. We went speeding down the runway, when at the last second, the driver saw the pilot standing in the middle of the runway with his parachute on. The driver swerved so hard it nearly threw me and another guy off the back of the truck. After that experience, we learned to hold on tight.

There were times when I talked with the pilots on the radio as they were coming in for a landing. I especially enjoyed this interaction. Other times, sitting thirty to forty feet from the runway, the jets would go by so fast I would get whiplash turning my head.

In 1966, I was assigned to the USS Noa 841 Destroyer, my home for the next three years along with about 300 other sailors. Each crew member was appointed to a certain duty station where he would have to go during an emergency call, such as going to battle or being under attack. This is called "general quarters." When any hint of danger happened, everybody scrambled to their specified place, which might not even be the area where he worked every day. My job was trainer on the gun mount. Once they sounded the alarm, I was required to get there as fast as I could.

The Noa was equipped with two sets of

5-inch, 38 caliber heavy guns, two sets of Mark 10/11 Hedgehogs (a projector-type weapon that throws 24 small projectiles several hundred feet ahead of the attacking vessel), six torpedo launchers, and eight nuclear-capable acoustic homing torpedoes. The Noa was not a big ship compared to others. She measured only 391 feet long and her steam turbine propulsion system enabled her to cruise at speeds above 30 knots. Living quarters were tight. The bunks were banked three high on each side. I was assigned a middle bunk and had a little over a foot of space overhead.

In the summer months, we wore white uniforms with the white Navy hat. During the winter, we were required to wear the heavy blue wool, which we didn't look forward to unless it was cold. We had a laundry facility on board. With our names stenciled on our clothes, they always came back to the right guy.

I never complained about the food. We always had a hot meal, unlike others on land.

My first two years I had a rough time. I felt like low class scum. Being an E-1 or E-2 made us everybody's whipping boys. We had to be at least an E-2 to go to sea.

During my first month or two aboard the Noa, I sat and stared out across the bow wishing I were home. After I got a bit of rank, things start changing for the better. Enlisted men's ranks start at E-1 up through E-9. I finally made E-4 during my tour of Vietnam.

Aboard the USS Noa, I became a third class boatswain's mate, bosun for short, the most versatile member onboard. We performed many tasks, such as maintenance, navigation, and supervising personnel assigned to the deck. We were also required to have general knowledge of ropes and cables. Boatswain's mates supervised and participated in damage control under combat conditions. In my position as gun mount and the only trainer on deck, I supervised a gun crew. My training and experience as a boatswain's mate served me well.

The first trip we took off the coast of North Carolina, we got caught in a storm. The ship bobbed up and down and rolled sideways. I never got seasick, but came close a number of times. With several others throwing up, the smell alone could make one heave.

Another time, while coming across the Atlantic from the Mediterranean Sea, I thought for sure we were in a hurricane. The waves were 40 to 60 feet high. We rode them up and then down into a big valley of water, called a trough.

I was at the helm. When the ship went up, then down and started back around, I spun the wheel as far right as it would go. The ship hit the bottom of the trough sideways. The waves were so huge I thought they were going to roll us. I slung the wheel back around to the other direction as hard as I could and held on. Everybody else piled into the right side. I was lying on the floor hanging onto the wheel and when the ship started coming back around, I managed to pull myself upright.

In a situation like that, a helmsman was not supposed to turn more than twenty-degrees without the officer in command giving the order. If he gave the command to go to full rudder, that's something like thirty to thirty-five degrees, we did it. If he didn't, it best not be done. Making that decision on the spot was scary, but I felt I had no choice. A sixty-foot wave is big enough to wash a plane off an aircraft carrier.

Afterward, nobody ever said anything to me about it. I was glad to be alive and I think everyone else was too.

My tour of Vietnam, counting the trip over and back, totaled nine months. When we went into ports to stock up on food and refuel we were allowed off ship. If we'd been out to sea an extra-long time, like a month, we could go ashore anywhere from three to five days, and that's when we got to see the countryside. We had shore leave in Hong Kong about every month to six weeks and also at the Subic Bay Naval Base in the Philippines.

At sea, we would sit a hundred yards or maybe several hundred feet off the beach shelling inland toward the airplanes, while sending out coordinates and firing over the hills or wherever. Those on the bridge might have known what we were shooting at but I never knew, nor did anybody down there with me know. When close to shore, we were not allowed on deck—the enemy could pop us off with a rifle.

Other times, I stood watch on the bridge, along with two guys on each side of the wings of the wheelhouse and a lookout on the back. I was in charge of that watch during my tour of Vietnam and in command of the several enlisted men.

I always enjoyed being on the bridge. I could see what was going on and knew what was happening, but not once did I see another ship while we were on patrol.

The scariest thing that ever happened when I was in Vietnam involved refueling. Sometimes we went into ports, other times we refueled at sea. In that case, an oil tanker came to us, making sure to keep its distance of anywhere from a hundred to a hundred and fifty feet between the two vessels. Any closer and we were likely to collide.

Our ship had three refueling stations located forward, amidships and aft. As second in command, I manned the front one, along with another guy, one rank above me, and a bunch of regular seamen in their first year or two.

With another tanker sitting to their port side, the crew threw us a rope and then a cable.

We pulled the rope over, then the cable next with the fuel line attached, securing each one in succession. Soon, we were in the final stages of hooking up everything. The hose was in the tank ready to pump when I looked up and saw the masts of the two tankers were not facing the same direction. I knew we were going to hit. The mast on the outside tanker started dropping back and coming in, and I knew it was fixin' to hit the tanker next to us and shove it into our ship.

I pointed to the mast. The guy in command of the fueling station saw it too. We ordered everyone to the opposite side of the ship. The tanker was coming in to hit us and hit us it did.

The E-5 guy in charge of the station and I had to go back around and cut everything lose. It wasn't so easy. Walking in oil at least one and a half to two feet deep, was like walking on ice.

The bosun, who thought he and I had to get it lose, proved to be no help at all. He hung onto the wall with both hands as the tanker kept hitting us, rolling away and back in, four or five times. Every time it hit, we'd look up and see parts falling from the mast. I had one hand on the wall holding onto a cleat. Hanging on by only that, I tried to beat the hook loose. But it was attached with a cotter key that took two hands to disconnect. Since I wasn't about to let go of the wall, I hung on until they sounded an emergency breakaway. When we pulled apart, the cable broke.

Those aboard the ship that hit us were angry about the cable, but there wasn't anything we could have done. Then again, we might have if the bosun in charge, an enlisted level E-5, had taken one hand off the wall and helped me. This is the first time I've told that story. Bosuns are tough—he just didn't act like one of the tough ones that day. He was scared to death, we both were. I wouldn't want to do it again.

During my four years in the Navy, I had the opportunity to see a lot of the world. I saw places along the Mediterranean and took tours to see the sites, especially in Athens and Rome. I traveled through the Panama Canal, a beautiful part of the world, and went to Hawaii twice. I saw a lot that I never dreamed was out there, North Africa, Southern Europe, Okinawa, and the Far East. I learned to eat rice with chopsticks in Japan. I didn't think there was any way possible I would learn to do that.

I had left for boot camp a week after my seventeenth birthday, just a kid. After being a sailor for four years, I came home a man. Things were different from when I left. I was now twenty-one and could go to the bars legally, but I had a rough time finding a job and getting started in life again.

There have been many times when I wished I'd stayed in the Navy and made it a career.

REMEMBERING THE GOOD PARTS

by Jay Harris

I lived in Clermont and attended Clermont High School. Following the completion of my freshman year in 1956, I enrolled in the Howey-in-the-Hills Academy where I graduated in 1960.

After graduation, I decided to join the U.S. Air Force and enlisted in September 1963. Following basic training, I was assigned to Amarillo Air Force Base where I attended school as a supply or logistics technician. My initial assignment following technical school was at the Tactical Air Command Base in Myrtle Beach, South Carolina, the summer of 1964.

After a little over two years of duty at Myrtle Beach Air Force Base, I received orders to report to a base in Spain. I was about to leave when everything stopped and I sat around for a couple of weeks waiting to ship out. Never getting a good reason for the delay, I volunteered for duty in Vietnam. In a couple of days, I was headed to Vietnam with a short stop in Japan for computer training.

Upon my arrival in Vietnam in September 1966, I was assigned to the 632nd Combat Support Group at Binh Thuy Air Base near the city of Can Tho in the Mekong Delta. This was a Vietnamese Air Force Base with USAF personnel assigned, and a U.S. Navy detachment nearby, along with U.S. Army forces in the area. Since there was a shortage of billeting (housing) on the base, I lived downtown in Can Tho.

I was in charge of data (computer) operations at the Squadron and had several Vietnamese women working for me. We all got along well and the operation ran smoothly.

Wanting to get more involved, I volunteered to teach English at a school in Can Tho. Vietnamese children and adults both attended the class. I enjoyed learning the customs and found helping the people rewarding.

There was a library in this school and one of the students noticed a wire extending out of a large book. I contacted the Air Force and someone came to check it out. He carefully opened the book whose pages had been hollowed out and removed. Inside he found an incendiary device that was within two hours of exploding. Had it detonated it would likely have killed many in the library and burned it to the ground.

When I wasn't working or teaching, a few of my buddies and I would occasionally borrow a jeep and explore the surrounding areas. Once we drove up almost to the Cambodian border. This was ill advised and dangerous. Getting caught would have resulted in disciplinary action. We were not in uniform, so not easily identifiable. Still, we managed to secure a couple of weapons. At one point, we came across some men working in the rice paddies. We didn't know if they were Viet Cong or if they were friendly.

Later, I asked one of my traveling companions what he would have done if they were the enemy.

He said, "I would have shot them."

I then told him we had no ammunition for the weapons.

I completed my tour in August 1967 and shipped back home. When I landed in the U.S., I heard some people yell, "You're a killer."

I ignored the heckling and thought of my off-duty work as a teacher and the good experiences I had in Vietnam. Can Tho suffered horribly during the TET offensive in 1969 and many of the beautiful buildings were destroyed or damaged. I prefer to remember them the way they were.

FEELINGS

Only Feelings

by Patrick McCrary

To be appointed leader of a squad of combat Marines is a promotion many Marines look forward to achieving. I've never met a Marine who wasn't ready to step forward and claim the responsibility of leadership. It's an inevitable advancement if you are serving your time as a squad member.

Vietnam was no different from the other wars fought by the brave men and women of our great country. Engaging the enemy is what it's all about, a situation a Marine would not likely miss, and he must find a way to be prepared. As time went by, the more experienced Marines would complete their required service time "in-country" and rotate back into the "world." We were trained to learn from those guys. The training we received as Marines was great, but no substitute for those who had already served in the war zone

On a very hot and humid day in South Vietnam, I received orders to lead my first patrol, appointed squad leader by virtue of seniority. I was in command of a squad of combat Marines. Show me someone who has a better job than that. I tell them to blow yer ass away and they will do it.

After being briefed on our patrol assignment by my platoon C.O., he instructed me to take along a new guy (FNG, fucking new guy) for our radioman. He needed the experience and we were not expecting any trouble.

Damn, lieutenants...I always expected trouble in Vietnam.

As my radioman and I assumed our position in the patrol column, I noticed a pair of binoculars around his neck. For the first time that day, I had a bad feeling. In Vietnam, anyone who carried extra gear worried me. Helmet, flak jacket, M-16, extra magazines and grenades, that was about all you needed. I sure didn't need to see thousands of meters away. Up close suited me just fine. After we had been out of the perimeter for about an hour, my fears began to materialize.

The radioman spotted a gook about two clicks (2000 meters) away with his binoculars. He then relayed the info to our platoon C.O. that he had an armed VC in sight.

Damn, that pissed me off. I mean—I was the squad leader. I'm supposed to assess the situation and decide if we need to report the contact. But that's what FNG did. Screwed things up. This time, the lieutenant was asking for me on the hook. For the second time that day, I had that bad feeling.

The lieutenant ordered me to move my squad toward the suspected VC and try to intercept, detain and question him. The damn gook was two thousand meters away. Not exactly a stroll through the park.

As we approached our objective, the gook was no longer in view. Why? I asked myself over and over as we tried to locate him. We were sitting ducks coming down that tree line and crossing the rice paddy. The entire countryside knew we were there by now. I hoped they had retreated thinking the rest of the platoon would be following us briefly.

All was secure as we began to search the village we had occupied. In the largest bunker, there was a cache of rice. A huge amount for that small of a village. I informed the lieutenant of our find and of the events that had occurred. He ordered me to destroy the rice with some explosives and to return to our perimeter.

After we fulfilled his orders, one of my fire team leaders suggested we stop at a footbridge we were familiar with that crossed a beautiful little stream in the area. We had been humping for hours now. A break would do us all good.

When we arrived at the footbridge, one could feel the coolness in the air. I instructed my fire team leaders to put out sentries on our flanks. It felt good to relax, tell ourselves what a great day it had been. It was a long hump and the destruction of the rice would cause problems for the VC in the coming months.

As I stressed earlier, there is no substitute for experience. It's like a sixth sense in regard to one's surroundings. Call it a gut reaction, call it what you will, because those feelings are as real as rain is wet. For the third time that day, I had a bad feeling. I could feel, hear, see, and notice the eerie silence. My God, I could have heard a pin drop. Shit. The hair stood at attention on the back of my neck. "Sentries in," I shouted. "Bret, get your fire team on the point and get us outta here. NOW!"

Everyone seemed stunned, probably thinking what's wrong with Mac.

I ordered, "Move, goddamn it. Saddle-up and move it outta here."

As everyone began to notice the problem, we moved with great haste toward the high ground that would provide us cover and access to the trail for our return to the rest of the platoon. We were only able to cover about half the distance when the Devil himself jumped up from out of the ground.

At least three AK-47s and several other weapons opened fire on us as we dove into the rice paddies seeking what little cover we could find. Other small firearms erupted from around our previous position. We had barely escaped. The enemy had circled us as we rested.

I made a quick assessment of our situation and found Doc, my corpsman, wounded from the opening round of rifle fire. Hit in the lower left leg, he was able to treat his own wound but wouldn't be able to move unaided. I instructed my radioman to get the platoon C.O. on the hook and advise him of our situation.

As the firefight progressed, I surmised we were in a bad position. The enemy could last a long time in this situation. When I finally got to the radio, my radioman had the lieutenant thinking we'd been overrun and half of us were dead.

What a guy. I made a request for an artillery fire mission in hopes of chasing the enemy away.

My platoon C.O. assured me he would get a fire mission in the works and for us to hold on. My two fire team leaders had spotted the enemy positions and were engaged in a furious firefight with them.

The VC getting the worst of it began to move into a low brushy area off our flank. Our M-79 (grenade launcher) man began to lob round after round into their position. We continued to take incoming rifle fire as the enemy fought back with all they had.

We had been engaged for over an hour and I was beginning to worry about our ammo. *Where was that artillery fire mission?*

I radioed the lieutenant and requested an immediate fire mission. I then moved along the paddy dike and instructed Lance Corporal Bret to get his fire team up and moving to the higher ground we had been approaching. We would provide cover for them and they could provide cover for the next fire team. We created a leapfrog escape from the open rice paddy. For the fourth time that day, I got another bad feeling.

The lieutenant came on the radio and informed me that a spotter round was incoming and to adjust our arty needs from the impact.

"Aye, aye, sir"

Bam! Loud explosion. A white phosphorous cloud appeared 50 meters from us. "Cease fire, cease fire," I screamed into the handset of the radio. "That spotter round is in our position, cease fire, damn it."

"Repeat your last," the radio crackled.

"Cease fire. We are getting low on ammo, and the enemy is hangin' tight. We need reinforcements. Now! Add 100 meters and give me three high explosives rounds."

The incoming automatic weapons fire was relentless. We had gotten the two fire teams out of the rice paddy, but Doc and I were still pinned down in that crossfire. About then the arty rounds began to arrive.

"All right, Doc ole buddy...it's me and you."

I grabbed him by his left arm and we ran three legged through the mud and machine gunfire. About every ten meters, we dove into the mud. I was amazed at his ability to endure the pain he must surely have been feeling. I suggested he take the morphine he carried, but he refused until his relief was present. Whenever we rose to move out, the gooks would open fire on us.

"Damn it." I cursed over and over.

Doc and I advanced along that paddy dike, ten meters or so at a time, until we were able to reach the relative safety of the rest of the squad.

God Bless those guys for providing cover fire.

The surprise over and now in a good position, we could pay full attention to the enemy.

Expending the last of our ammo, the rest of the platoon began moving into our position. After we got the corpsman, a medivac incoming, we moved out to search the area for the enemy. Once again, they had disappeared as they so often did in Nam.

Thinking back on that day, I can really see how through the ages, Marines have gotten so protective of their corpsman. The only one wounded, he uttered not a word of discouragement. That corpsman upheld the highest traditions of the United States Naval services. He made me proud to serve beside him.

The FNG's M-16 took a round through the stock, but that didn't count as a wound.

After evacuating the corpsman, I recounted to my platoon sergeant how I had those four bad feelings. That I felt like I had nearly caused the deaths of brave Marines. Four mess ups on my part as a new squad leader was a near disaster.

To my amazement he said, "Mac, you're gonna be good at this. Feelings are for a reason but they are only feelings. It's the

Marines who react to them, who keep their men alive. It's what you do about those feelings that count. Go get your squad set in for the night."

I'll never be able to describe the way I felt at that moment, but I'll say...I was very lucky to be in the presence of a brave, wise and honorable Marine.

God Bless the brave men of the 2nd Squad, 2nd Platoon, A Company, 1st Battalion, 5th Marine Regiment, 1st Marine Division.

God Bless the Marine Corps.

GUNG HO

(One of the first, but not the last)

by Joe Koester

I graduated from Clermont High School in 1959. With a draft card in hand, I was expected to serve in the military. I had vague thoughts of enlisting in the Marines, Navy or Air Force, in no particular order.

Bill Morse and I were working at the Clermont 66 Service Station at the corner of Highway 50 and 5th Street in 1960, when he said, "I'm thinking about going into the Air Force. You wanna go too?"

When the Air Force recruiter came by to talk with Bill, I remember saying the fateful words "Hey, Sarge, have you got a place in there for me?"

We went to Orlando for some testing and were apparently successful as we were soon headed to Jacksonville to be sworn in. There were the two of us from Clermont and a fellow from Leesburg headed off to Lackland Air Force Base for basic training while the other 30 or 40 were going in the Army. After basic, Bill and I went our separate ways.

I headed to Goodfellow Air Force Base in San Angelo, Texas for eight months, training as an intelligence analyst. After graduation, I was assigned to the 6981st Radio Group Mobile at Elmendorf Air Force Base in Anchorage, Alaska.

During the last part of technical school, my father died and I tried to get an assignment closer to Florida. When that didn't happen, I swapped assignments with another fellow and went to the 6984th Security Squadron at Shemya Air Force Station at the western tip of the Aleutian Islands. I was stationed on a two by four mile island for one year, and then went to the 6989th Security Squadron at Misawa Air Base in Northern Japan.

While at Misawa, the Air Force was sending some personnel on temporary duty (TDY) to Vietnam. Unfortunately, for me, they were only sending Russian Linguists and did not need any Intelligence Analysts.

I completed my two-year tour in Japan and four years, four months and one day after enlisting I was a civilian again.

In 1966, I applied for a position with the National Security Agency in the Washington DC area, was accepted and began a career there. After additional training, I worked in an analytical element, watching things heat up in Vietnam.

Later, I learned that NSA was sending civilians over to staff a Cryptologic Support Center at MACV Headquarters in Saigon. I applied for that position as well, and again was accepted, and arrived in-country March 1969.

At that time, our presence was covert, and we had people in various locations supporting military units and commands. I primarily supported the MACV J2 (Intelligence) and my area of responsibility and expertise was I Corps, in the DMZ area in northern South Vietnam. My Intelligence support was primarily for the Army and the Marine Corps units.

Although I was a civilian, I wore a uniform with no military insignia and had DOD SPEC REP (Department of Defense, Special Representative) MACV on my uniform. I carried a weapon, ate GI food and lived in a Bachelor Officer's Quarters (BOQ) in Saigon and in barracks while up country.

I was quite gung ho as I had seen too many John Wayne movies and wanted to get my licks in. While I was never in combat, I was under fire a couple of times, and started questioning my sanity for "volunteering" for this. I was in-country about three months when I came to the realization that "we" were never going to "win" this thing and had no business in Vietnam. I remembered arguing with a wise old Navy chief back in Maryland about Vietnam and turned out, he was right.

While my opinions about my country's presence in Vietnam had changed, my support for the military never faltered. Realizing many of my fellow comrades had the same feelings, I continued to do my best to support them. It was with pride that I worked many 12-hour shifts helping to locate enemy forces and protect our troops. I do not regret serving my year in Vietnam and returned home safely in March 1970.

I had a rewarding career with the National Security Agency and many of my various jobs were providing support to our military services. I have over 15 years of experience with Middle Eastern targets and I retired from my last position with USAF's Air Intelligence Agency in San Antonio, Texas in December 1998.

In January of 1999, I moved to Tennessee and enjoyed retirement until 9/11. Then I volunteered at Headquarters and was back at work November 2001. I worked there for four months, and although given the opportunity to stay indefinitely, I chose to return to retirement.

In September 2002 I received a call from Headquarters asking if I would come back to work with the Army at Fort Gordon, Georgia. They said I would have to do about four weeks of training at Fort Gordon, but it took me six weeks to become marginally proficient in seven different computer systems. I completed this training and came back home to await a call to report for duty that came in February 2003.

I went back to working 12-hour shifts supporting our military operations in Kuwait and Iraq. Once again, I did not support the political decision that put our troops in Iraq, but I did support our military forces wherever they might be placed in harm's way. I stayed there until we were in Baghdad and the need for what I was doing had changed. I was offered a position in another area, but declined. I then resigned my position and returned to retirement, this time for good.

I was pleased to learn I was the fourth most productive intelligence analyst/reporter in the Iraqi cell while stationed there. And, I am proud and honored to have worked with and for our military in that situation and in all the other positions I served while in the military or as a civilian intelligence analyst. I would not change anything if I had a chance to do it again.

THE TIME

by Patrick McCrary

"Now is the time for all good men to come to the aid of their country." A great line with humble beginnings, by a teacher named Charles Wilder that carries a profound message. The phrase was introduced to me in a high school typing class. Had only I known in a few short years I would have men greater than I, show me what the message meant.

I, as well as all the men I knew in the Marine Corps, volunteered to come to the aid of our country. I did so with pride. I wanted to go to Vietnam, to help repulse the evil forces of communism. However, when I arrived in Vietnam and began the fight, I was scared to death most of the time, brave every now and then, and lucky to have survived the enemy's best efforts to kill me. Most of all I was fortunate to have been led by men who truly loved their corps, as well as the men they led. It seemed no sacrifice was too great. Still, I often found myself longing to be back in typing class at dear old Clermont High.

I recall a time where one of those men showed me, by example, what the message of coming to the aid of my country meant.

It was early February 1969. I had just made corporal and appointed the platoon's right guide. A great job to have when part of a combat group in Vietnam. Platoon Sergeant Rios and I, our tour of duty in Nam almost over, would soon be rotating back to the world. We only had three weeks left and our replacements would be arriving any day.

We had lost our lieutenant earlier in January. A new lieutenant, fresh out of Officer Basic was with us now and a new platoon sergeant on the way. Any of the guys could fill my job. Still, the platoon was going to be in a world of hurt for some solid leadership. Sergeant Rios had trained new guys before and was doing an excellent job, but time was short. Much to teach in so little time.

The morning of February 6, 1969, we

were in the Arizona Territory of the An Hoe basin, in South Vietnam. We left the company perimeter, ordered into an area known to be heavily mined and booby-trapped. I knew in my heart Sgt. Rios would have advised against such a move.

The area was too dangerous to patrol on foot, especially with one platoon, one radioman, one corpsman, one battle-hardened sergeant and one shiny, new lieutenant.

Dang! Something wasn't adding up. No one in the bush would have sent us into an area like that. Battalion had to have ordered this patrol.

Approaching the edge of the high ground that would lead us to our objective, Sgt. Rios gave us a break in a village we had come upon.

I've talked about men who loved their corps and their country but I haven't talked about my hatred of the Viet Cong. Now is a good time.

These villagers were different than most of the rural Vietnamese. They were well-fed, not skin and bones like most others. *Well-fed and living on the edge of a dangerous area.* The hair stood on the back of my neck and I was tingling all over. *They are the ENEMY.* Everything I had learned told me to kill them. But, most of the time, when you saw the VC, he was unarmed.

We had searched the area and found nothing. Sgt. Rios and the lieutenant made plans for us to move on. The grunts could tell something good was happening. I smiled as we gathered the villagers and put them on the point. Want to boost morale? Put a human minesweeper on the point. About ten of them. If there was a mine or booby trap they would avoid it, and get us to where we were going safely.

I saw the fear in the eyes of the enemy as we motioned them, at rifle point, up the hill, in the lead. Although we knew where we were going, the villagers didn't. Our point fire team leader was doing the best he could when the crest of the hill turned into a boxed area that split off in several directions. He was at a loss as to which direction to proceed.

I was at the end of the patrol wondering what was holding us up. Hearing the radio crackle, I knew a delay of some sort had occurred and the lieutenant would have to give new orders. Then I saw Sgt. Rios beginning to pick his way past the grunts in the point fire team to reach the front and direct our movements.

Typical, I was thinking—Sgt. Rios is going where the lieutenant should be going. I turned, facing outboard into the brush, to detect any enemy movement, when an explosion nearly caused me to lose my breath. I wheeled around and looked at the origin of the sound where Sgt. Rios had been a split second before. I caught a glimpse of a helmet shooting straight up about 40 to 50 meters off the ground. Marines turned and ran from the dust and smoke where the explosion originated.

I couldn't believe it. Twenty people had been over that spot in the last ten minutes. *How?* The radio crackling to life around me, I began to make my way up the hill to assist in the evacuation and medivac. I was passing some of the bravest men I had ever known, their faces drawn and eyes hollow. I reached the second team leader, Lance Corporal Britt and asked, "Who?"

Avoiding eye contact, he replied, "Papa Sierra" (platoon sergeant).

My knees weakened, but my pace quickened. "Damn it to hell," I said. My worst fears were realized as I arrived and began to help the corpsman with Sgt. Rios.

Sgt. Rios had stepped on a mine or had become the victim of a command detonation. Both of his legs were vaporized in an instant. His right arm was held on only by a few severely torn muscles, skin, and bone. His rifle had acted as a guillotine nearly severing his arm from the force of the explosion. His left hand torn in several places.

On the verge of eruption, my eyes clouded over as the corpsman completed tying off the tourniquets. The corpsman couldn't get a good vein for an IV. He had to use his K-Bar knife to cut into Sgt. Rios's left wrist to find a vein so he could begin to administer the life sustaining solution. The radioman was giving coordinates for the medivac.

The world seemed to come to a stop. When I looked up the trail in the direction we were headed, I saw the enemy squatting in their familiar ass-on-the-ground, knees under their armpits. Several of their eyes met mine. Their mouths began to open, slowly at first, and then they must have seen my anger. I raised my M-16 to my shoulder and took aim. I flipped the selector switch to full automatic. The "gooks" began to chatter and extend their arms up in a show of surrender.

Damn their sorry asses. Damn their souls to hell. My finger slacked off the trigger, when I felt a hand on my flak jacket. It was the corpsman.

"The medivac chopper is inbound; let's get Sarge to the LZ."

Four of us, the corpsman, Lance/Cpl Britt, Lance/Cpl Stuckinsmit and myself, Cpl McCrary, each grabbed a corner of the poncho, used it as a stretcher and carried Sergeant Vince Rios to the LZ for transport to 1st Hospital Company, Da Nang. I was filled with dread. Sarge had lost both his legs. Probably would lose his right arm. His left hand mangled badly. I was afraid he would lose his life before they could get him to the Surgeons in Da Nang—a full 30 minutes by chopper.

As the C46 medivac chopper lifted into the clear afternoon sky, I reflected on how much Sgt. Rios meant to us. His leadership had saved my life several times. He always gave first choice to his grunts for cigarettes and C-rations. He never took any new gear unless it was going to be sent back on a resupply. He took the last choice for radio watch every night. Now—he might lose his life in a miserable third-world country that didn't give a damn about him.

In a moment of clarity, I realized Sgt. Rios hadn't lost anything. He gave, as he always had, his legs and his arm trying to ensure others would live. He gave, to his men, to his corps, to his country. He would be the one who was greater than me, who gave the true meaning of that familiar sentence. *Now is the time for all good men to come to the aid of their country.*

For this act of bravery and compassion on February 6, 1969, Sergeant Vince Rios, United States Marine Corps, was awarded his second Bronze Star (w/combat V device) his third Purple Heart Medal, and the everlasting love of his platoon. It was an honor to serve with someone who showed what the title "United States Marine" really stood for.

Semper Fidelis
Patrick "Mac" McCrary

WELCOME TO VIETNAM

by Ted Cook

Most new Army arrivals to Vietnam came through Tan Son Nhut Airbase, and then to a replacement company before reaching the unit they were assigned or had requested them. I was sent to the 25th Infantry Division's Military Police Company since that was my MOS (Military Occupational Specialty).

Stepping off the large jet in January 1969 was like walking back into Clermont, Florida, weather—hot and wet with no breeze. Troops would usually catch a truck to their new unit, but my division was at Cu Chi, 30 miles away. Since there had been daylight activity from our little friends, we were ushered onto three

Chinooks for the short ride, a twenty-five minute flight.

As we approached the helo pad in Cu Chi, the crew chief made an announcement. "There is some activity in the woods beyond the end of the runway. Nothing to worry about. We get this all the time, just smoke and mirrors."

When we touched down, the back door opened and we were told to exit quickly because the chopper was taking off as soon as we had "un assed." We started at a leisurely pace until the crew chief yelled, "Move your asses."

Explosions about 100 meters away seemed to be coming our way. Some guys actually stopped to look, causing a real problem until shrapnel from the mortars started hitting the aircraft hulls.

Later, I found out the explosions were caused by 50-mm mortars that a person can hold like a pipe between their legs. They will do a lot of damage with a direct hit. Most were falling without real direction, and then they started falling much closer. No time for a bunker, we were instructed to take cover behind a wall (revetment) and someone would come get us.

After an all-clear sounded, we were gathered together and someone said, "Welcome to Vietnam, gentlemen. There will be more of the same. Now move your asses." An all too familiar phrase I would hear numerous times during my tour of Vietnam.

What we experienced was harassment fire from the local VC in the villages about five kilometers from the field. Two months later, the village was destroyed in a major fight.

After arriving in Vietnam in mid-January '69, I attended RVN (Republic of Vietnam) Orientation, designed for personnel involved with field operations. The attendees included EOD (explosive ordnance devices) specialist, engineers, infantry soldiers, artillery and military police, which I was. The school was an eight-day course in everything we would have covered in infantry training such as fire and maneuver, helicopter dismount, mines and booby traps (how to recognize and leave alone), plus tunnel school. The 25th Division had the Cu Chi tunnels inside the camp and we were required to go through them as part of the course.

The last day included live fire exercises. Four soldiers descended into in a six-foot-deep pit and then firing overhead commenced using several different weapons: an M-16, a Chinese 7.62 machine gun, an AK47, and a SKS Soviet rifle. Each possesses a different sound. The purpose of the exercise was for us to distinguish the difference and be better prepared for what we might encounter.

Once in the hole and the firing began, I found it interesting until the NCO with us got a strange look on his face. We were catching fire from another direction. Turned out some VC were taking advantages of our exercise to stage a small infiltration since these training sessions always occurred at the same time each day.

We waited out the first few rounds and then made a break for the road behind us, looking for the closest shelter, about 50 meters away. As we were getting out of the pit, mortar rounds started falling around us. I yelled to the artillery troops and engineers in my group to head for cover in the tunnels we had just been through. The fire lasted probably five minutes but seemed longer. Then we heard a gunship overhead. The mortars stopped and we hit the road.

The following day as the school's session ended, we were pleased no one was injured. However, upon returning to duty the next day, I got my butt chewed out by the provost marshal (a colonel), the company commander and my platoon sergeant. The best thing I heard about that day was "well at least the new guy doesn't have his head in his ass." Then I got a commendation. Go figure.

I had been on a convoy security detail for about six weeks and all had been somewhat quiet after the Dau Tieng attacks in February. On March 11, 1969 at a checkpoint, the convoy planned to split into two groups, one to Tay Ninh and the other to Dau Tieng. After clearing several checkpoints, it looked like we would have an uneventful run. Nevertheless, as we went through the last village usual civilian activity disappeared. We started taking a lot of fire from a wood line about fifty meters to our right, then sporadic shots from the village on our left. When this happened, we cranked things up and ran through as best we could.

My crew and I got through with only a couple of holes in the fenders of the jeep and all but two of the trucks made it. We were the last group in the convoy except for the trailing party, the wreckers and two extra tractors for towing disabled vehicles. I could see the damaged trucks, one from a rocket-propelled grenade launchers (RPG), and one because the driver had been hit and hurt enough that he was hiding in the cab. Since these guys were our responsibility, the crew and I turned around and went back.

I instructed my gunner to concentrate on the wood line and I would take the village side with our driver doing the maneuvering. We got to the first truck, grabbed the driver, then to the second truck and picked up that driver. About that time, the colonel, our provost marshal flying overhead, came over the radio and asked if I could mark where I thought the fire originated.

In response, I tossed a smoke grenade as far as I could toward the woods and told him anything east of the smoke was where I thought the enemy was positioned.

The village fire had stopped at that point.

There was a Cobra along with the colonel and as we left, he started his first run. It took three and I guess the VC decided to leave. I left the uninjured driver with the trailing party, and took the injured one with me, dropping him at the base hospital in Tay Ninh.

Afterwards, the convoy regrouped and headed back to Cu Chi to start another day.

It was amazing that this whole affair lasted about an hour but it felt like three. Later, I was required to write an after-action report about the event. What a pain in the ass that was!

After the March hit on our resupply group, the MP Company formed a new platoon for tactical operations. This group was made up of MP sergeants, other enlisted MPs and several infantry personnel who had gotten out of the field because of purple hearts, took two or three, and a new platoon leader, who was infantry and with the same reason for getting out of the field. I was transferred to this group and we started small unit tactics training consistent with the job. MPs were combat support and law enforcement—not infantry, although we served in that capacity from time to time.

During this time, we continued our convoy duties and served as a reaction force group to plug any holes in the wire following rocket or mortar attacks.

In May, June, and July, camp Cu Chi experienced several rocket attacks as well as four attempts to breach the wire between bunkers more than twenty-five meters apart. Joe M. caught two VC coming through on the northeast side. He killed one and injured another, who we took as a prisoner. John Br. caught three in separate incidents, killing one and wounding two in the exchange of gunfire. I wounded three close to our barracks near the wire. After that, things quieted down for several weeks until September 20, 1969.

During one of our routine missions, we had passed several checkpoints without incident and headed to the area where the convoy would split. I was in the group headed toward Dau Teing that day. On the final leg of our journey, there was this road that ran through the Michelin rubber plantation. The trees had been cleared about fifty meters away. That in itself seemed suspicious. Also, there was no traffic, always a bad sign. About a klick past the turnoff, we started taking fire from the tree line and several mortar rounds fell behind us. The unit ahead of me had passed through some heavy small arms and a couple of RPGs.

Approaching a quad 50s (four .50 caliber machine guns mounted together on the back of a truck), we spied movement to their right flank. My gunner and I took some shots and the movement stopped. I dropped several M-79 rounds in the area to make sure. Our unit made it, but was recalled to the contact area to assist the infantry in clearing the road and pick up any stragglers.

We then continued on to Tay Ninh, met up with our lieutenant and went back to base camp at Cu Chi. After we left, the NVA attempted to close both roads to Tay Ninh and Dau Teing. Groups from the 3/22, 2/12, and 2/27 put a stop to this, and I understand everything went well from then on.

A week later, I was sent to Tay Ninh to replace an NCO going home.

After being assigned to Tay Ninh, security escorts were the same, just smaller. We were running to different firebases without a whole convoy. The biggest change was that I became involved with supervision of indigenous personnel. All of the laborers and cleanup crews came through the main gate with an ID and were then picked up by their respective units that had employed them. If they wandered outside their assigned area, they were tossed off base.

Tay Ninh was considered an "open city" because the seat of the Cao Dai religion was located there and they had their own army to defend the faithful. The NVA left them alone and the city as well. We patrolled the area as we would any other place, but with a little more caution. Open cities attracted black markets and we ran across two of them by watching what went out of the main gate and who was doing the transporting.

We had set up a checkpoint a klick beyond the main gate where the transports entered the city and another two on the other side. As expected, the participants in the black market, who were American civilians, met with their contacts, two AWOLs living in the city, and we surprised them. The civilians were pissed but didn't offer any resistance, as they were associated with the CIA. The others, who were Army and going to jail, decided to fight. They took a couple of shots but returned buckshot convinced them to surrender. That put a stop on those ops for a while.

The CIA personnel were transferred and we got a new group to put up with, the U.S. AID (Agency for International Development).

I left on R&R to Sidney in November '69.

I returned to Tay Ninh and Cambodia in late January where I served my remaining time. Nothing had changed in convoy security since the last tour here, but we had a new emphasis on an old job—supervising the searches of the indigenous personnel for contraband, bandages, medical supplies, and food unavailable on the regular market. Apparently, there was a lot of classified material from brigade headquarters unaccounted for and leaving through individuals working as cleaners. We changed the search procedures and stopped that.

The worst thing about Tay Ninh was our location, only twelve kilometers from the Cambodian border and subject to frequent rocket and mortar fire. Sometimes, they were pretty accurate. In February and

March, rockets got the PX, a fuel storage tank, a small ammunition dump site, and the airfield three times, knocking out a few Cobras. There were also several probes of the camp during this time but they were repelled with few casualties, no KIAs (Killed in Action).

Since our unit was located on the west side, any of the rounds that fell short hit pretty close. We could hear the shrapnel hitting the roofs and the sides of the buildings. At the end of March, one of these attacks took out two of our barracks and the mess hall. All personnel were on duty or in bunkers at the time so we didn't lose anyone. Afterwards, we moved across the base to an area that the Filipinos had vacated. It was much nicer than what we were used to.

At about this time, large amount of supplies began to disappear, so we started following the trucks as they left base. We ended up catching a group of mostly Korean civilians dealing in black market items. They were part of a group that ran the generators for the camp and thought they were above suspicion. Their scheme ended when several of them were sent back to Korea.

On May 1, 1970, my squad and two others escorted a group of officers, engineers and supply trucks moving northeast to a firebase called Katum, two kilometers from Cambodia. Once an old French outpost, it had been built up and included an airfield. Our group was assigned to secure the airfield's west side. There were no bunkers, just a short berm bulldozed by the engineers to separate us from the woods.

We were fortunate to have three M-60s as part of our usual armament, because over the next two weeks there were three attempts to damage the airfield. With additional firepower and support from the Cobra gunships, we were able to prevent that from happening.

Later, we moved to another firebase near the border where we met some bridging engineers whom we escorted to a village almost on the border so they could construct a bridge across a small river. While there, we started receiving fire from across the border. We were able to return enough fire with our M-60s to allow the engineers to finish the bridge—just in time for a group of APCs (Armored Personnel Carriers) from 4/23 Mechanized Infantry to cross and drive off whoever was shooting at us.

The first week of June, my unit returned to Tay Ninh. The operation was coming to a close and I had only two months left. Rocket fire had subsided for about five weeks, a welcomed reprieve.

The week before I was to go home, we had our first major injury in six months. A guy from California was sleeping when we got a rash of incoming mortar fire. Scott was in his bunk when a round came through the tin roof and exploded six feet from his bed. He wasn't killed, but it almost cut him in two. One of the guys got our three-quarter ton truck, then we loaded him bed and all into the truck, and drove to the 45th surgical hospital where they were able to stabilize him. The next day Scott was sent to Japan.

I spent my remaining six days in a highly agitated state before leaving Tay Ninh on September 5, 1970. My trip home included a stop at Division HQ in Cu Chi and then to Oakland Army base and finally home.

My tour of Vietnam was finally behind me, but like many of my comrades, the memories of those days still linger no matter how hard we try to forget.

BAD DREAMS

by Patrick McCrary

Crossing a rice paddy was never a lot of fun, especially if it was large. Let's face it, my platoon was out in the open with nowhere to take cover except in the mud. Incoming rifle fire has the right of way and if you had to, then it was splat, face first into the mud and water buffalo crud. The VC used this as a harassment technique. They'd open fire with AK-47s and watch the Marines drink rice paddy water.

One hot and humid August afternoon in Vietnam, our platoon had point, which means we were the first in the column. We were crossing a large rice paddy and as we approached the far side, all hell broke loose. Several of the enemy opened fire as we approached their village. We took cover as best we could in that open paddy and returned fire as only Marine riflemen can. Then the order came down to cease fire and pull back.

Pull back? Marines never pull back. Not to mention it was a long way back across that rice paddy.

About then, a roar came out of the sky that put a smile on our faces. Phantoms. The F-4s, the *baddest* aircraft in the sky. Pull back? Hell YES! As the Jet Jocks did their thing, we watched with enthusiasm, anticipating the upcoming search of the flattened village that dared to attack us. *Pay with your lives you VC fools. We have our company commander with us today and he has the power to unleash the Devil's Fury on you.*

As the Phantoms finished their bombing runs, we were on the rice paddy dikes and almost running toward the village. We weren't the only ones. We began to notice that civilians from the surrounding areas were also running to the flattened village.

What had happened? Why all the other villagers?

When we entered the devastated village, combat ready, and prepared to kill anything that moved, it became apparent something was terribly wrong. The screaming began. The wailing of old women, the shouts and cries of old men. Where were the dead VC? Where were the bastards who dared to attack us? My God, what had happened?

Thirty minutes ago, we were in a firefight for our lives. Bomb craters were everywhere, but only one found its way into history. A five hundred pound high explosive had scored a direct hit on one of the village bunkers. Six children, none older than eight years old, and four adults, all over fifty, were dead. Why? Because of a few chicken shit VC snipers and because Marines attack when attacked—we were warriors at war.

Fate dealt a terrible hand that day. A few VC snipers and a few brave Marines had caused the death of many harmless people. I wondered...Oh God, why do the little ones have to suffer because of the foolish mistakes of adults?

I looked down in the bunker at an old woman cradling a lifeless child. Both dead, with more children at her feet. Dead, all dead.

The bomb had cut the bunker in half. Body parts were scattered in the crater. A large wooden beam had severed one of the victim's body in half and crushed a child's skull. There were no survivors.

As more and more relatives of the dead arrived on the scene, the wailing became unbearable. I was so overwhelmed, I froze in place, watching the horror unfold before my eyes. I couldn't get those dead kids out of my mind. The whole scene was the stuff bad dreams are made of. As the more able-bodied locals began to dig the remains out of the rubble, I had the most terrible feeling of utter helplessness and hopelessness. I could serve no purpose there.

Official Report: Ten VC killed in action during firefight and resulting air strike.
Eye Witness Report: Six children and four elderly civilians, dead.
The victims of someone else's actions.

My platoon searched the area on the outskirts of the village and in the first sweep; we found a large cache of rifles and ammunition buried on a sand bar in the bend of a small stream that flowed through there. At least we knew the enemy was among them, but to this day, I think the enemy was us.

THIRTEEN MONTHS

My Life in Vietnam

by Robert L. Jones

My name is Bobby Jones. I graduated from Clermont High School in 1966 and enlisted in the Marine Corps that same year. It's hard for me to write about my time in Vietnam because we weren't supported by our country. We were just doing what was asked of us. When I came back, I wouldn't fly across the US in uniform even though the airlines would have let me fly free. I didn't want anyone to know I was in the Marines, let alone coming home from Vietnam.

The other thing about telling my story is that I don't want to sound like I'm bragging.

Every serviceman or woman makes a sacrifice, no matter where they are told to go or where they become stationed. That being said, here we go...

I volunteered for the Marine Corps feeling certain I would end up going to Vietnam. Regardless of what branch of the service I went into, I thought I might get better survival training in the Corps. I did my basic training at Paris Island, South Carolina, ITR (Infantry Training Regiment) at Camp Lejeune, North Carolina, Communications School in San Diego, and finally, stationed at Camp Pendleton, California.

On July 29, 1967, I shipped out to Vietnam as a member of the Ninth Marines, Third Division, and spent most of my time near or on the Demilitarized Zone. The DMZ was a three-mile wide strip of land on either side of the Ben Hai River that acted as a buffer between North and South Vietnam. I never stayed in a safe area and was always subjected to incoming artillery, rockets and mortars as well as small arms fire.

As a field wireman in communications with infantry units, I laid communications wire, two-stranded, between defensive positions on the DMZ and in all the forward combat bases. These included Con

Thien, Gio Linh, Cam Lo, C-2, Dong Ha, Ca Lu and other remote locations.

We were located on the north side of the Dong Ha Bridge where there was always a tremendous amount of combat activity. Marines were often coming down from Gio Lin with a large North Vietnamese Army (NVA) force in pursuit.

Fellow Marines were being killed and wounded all the time. I can still see the dead bodies on tanks during the TET offensive in 1968. I started thinking about the families of the dead Marines who didn't yet know that their son, dad, husband, or brother would not be coming home alive. I thought how heartbroken they would be when told, and how they wouldn't understand why their loved one had to die.

Today, when I hear of a service person getting killed, all I can think about is their family's sorrow.

When I was at the Cam Lo Village, we were hit by a large force of the NVA. There were so many NVA killed that the Seabees came in with bulldozers, dug holes and pushed all the dead into the holes. That night, two Marines were under a truck that was hit with a rocket-propelled grenade (RPG) round that blew up the truck and burned the Marines.

Burning flesh and hair is a smell I'll

never forget. Sleeping is difficult at times, because even now, I cannot get those images and smells out of my head.

While in Vietnam, most of us did not want to get close to anyone, we didn't want to know their personal life, their girlfriend's name or anything else. It made it easier if anything happened. However, I did develop an enduring friendship with a special buddy. At the time, I was just a private and Steve was a corporal. Like I said earlier— best not to make friends with anybody, but we did.

A lot of people would die in the first month or two because they didn't know how to take care of themselves. I'd been there a couple of months and felt like I knew how to stay alive. When Steve came over, I took him under my wing. Like me, he survived and now lives in Delaware. We've stayed in contact and have this ongoing argument: I often kid him about how I saved his life, and he kids me back and says, "No, I saved yours."

During one of our operations on the DMZ, command wanted landline communications between our outposts and the big gun up at C-2, a naval cannon removed from a Navy ship. It was a big gun with a barrel sixteen inches in diameter. They wanted radio communications between that gun and our outposts on the DMZ. They also wanted wire laid.

Steve and I installed a landline from C-2 to Con Thien. This was the first ground communications ever put in on the DMZ. Besides installing it, we had to maintain it during Operation Lancaster, which spanned a three-month period. We started at the gun in the morning and followed the landline to Con Thien. This was ten or fifteen miles down a dirt road. Every morning we got up and checked that line, knowing we might be ambushed or find a land mine or a booby trap planted for us.

In the beginning, it was hard to handle emotionally, but after a while it became routine work.

One day, we had a new guy helping. We were going along the landline and saw a place where the line went underground. Steve and I knew we didn't bury it underground, but the new guy didn't. He grabbed hold of the landline and was ready to jerk it up. Steve and I went for him and the wire to get him off it before he blew us all up.

We made it through that event, and at the time, we even thought it funny. Looking back, it wasn't funny at all.

At night, we stayed at Con Thien. The next day we got up and followed the line back to C-2, repairing it and making sure it was okay. That was our job for a couple of months.

By the time we returned to Dong Ha, we were exhausted. At first, we slept on the ground, but eventually we constructed some huts. Built on platforms about two to three feet high made them susceptible to incoming fire. I didn't feel safe sleeping in the huts, so Steve and I dug out one of the nearby trenches, adding enough space to sleep in with some comfort.

Back at Dong Ha, where the Ninth Marine regiment was stationed, there was an airbase and airstrip, and every now and then the Army would come in. Steve and I, being in communications, were in charge of wire, switchboards and everything, always made sure that a lineman was scheduled to show up around lunchtime, so we'd get to eat with them. The Army had hot food, much better than our C-rations.

When TV reporters from the US came over, I refused to be interviewed. Our country was so divided, I didn't want anybody stateside to know I was there. While the reporters were conducting interviews, we could hear the firefights going on.

This also took place when we were running those landlines we had to maintain. Sometimes snipers would be waiting; therefore, we always had a squad along to protect us.

While in Vietnam, I found it hard to talk to people, and just as hard when I got home. There were things that happened—things I don't want to remember, but can't forget. I know three or four people from my regiment whose names are on "The Wall." I wasn't a ground fighter, so I didn't know many people personally who were fighting on the ground. Day in and day out, their world consisted of a ten-man squad.

With me being in a regiment, working with all these different companies, I never tried to get to know any of them. There's no telling how many people I saw over there who didn't make it back, and I didn't even know their names. A lot of times, we didn't use your real name. Instead, you had a nickname. My good friend, Steve, from Delaware named me Bones because I was a skinny little kid.

I found myself, like so many others, fighting in a war that few of us understood. We were doing something that as Americans we felt we should do because our government asked us to.

I was an eighteen-year-old kid—I wasn't going to question what our President asked, though perhaps I would today.

We weren't supposed to cross that DMZ—though we did. We knew where their camps were, but we couldn't go after them.

We had to sit and wait for them to come after us.

The Marine Corps trained us to be aggressive. Our job was to take out the enemy. But, the Vietnam War wasn't like WWI or WWII where everybody wanted to defeat the enemy and the country supported them. Instead, we had to wait for the enemy to open fire, meaning somebody would die, and then we could retaliate.

For thirteen months that was my life and I feel fortunate to have come home physically intact. But, when I see or talk with Vets who didn't, I am consumed with guilt.

I have had difficulties in my life that I didn't realize, until a few years ago, were a result of my experiences in Vietnam. When I came home after being discharged, I never talked about Vietnam to non-Vets. I thought being withdrawn was normal. I continued the isolation I had started there, and it has hurt me in relationships. Those thirteen months will stay with me for the rest of my life.

TOUR OF DUTY

Inside the Wire

by Ron Brooks

I have spent the last forty-five years trying not to remember details of my Vietnam experience. First of all, I was not so brave. I was a scared teenage kid from small town America who had never even seen a bad traffic accident. Personally, I prefer to keep the ugly, darker parts tucked away, but I'll make an effort to write my story "Inside the Wire."

During the Vietnam War, most U.S. Army companies in-country conducted assignments off base referred to as "Outside the Wire." Sooner or later, while conducting these missions, they were going to end up in a firefight. Some with heavy combat, others brief encounters, over within minutes. At first, we didn't know, but soon figured out we were engaged with the North Vietnamese Army (NVA), Viet Cong (VC), or both.

Well trained and equipped, the NVA surpassed others at taking an area, building bunkers, and defending their position. The VC, not as well trained, were well known for guerilla warfare, surprise attacks, ambush, hit and run tactics, and booby traps. They were also very good at blending in with the local civilian population.

Most veterans have multiple stories of combat actions, some horrible, frightful, and even appalling. Some feel those memories are better off tucked away in the back of your mind and not talked about. Although, other Vets say they feel better if they talk about their experiences to clear the air. Then there are those who say after forty-five years they still get emotional, tear up, and feel depressed for days after dredging up those dark days. Today, these guys would be diagnosed with PTSD.

If you think a base camp is considered a safe zone—think again. I was assigned to one just outside the Iron Triangle and the

Ho Bo Woods, approximately twenty-five miles north of Saigon. The VC were supported by and fought alongside the NVA to ensure control of the area. Vast networks of tunnels were constructed in the Iron Triangle area, reaching down into the hamlet of Cu Chi. This entire area was considered a hornet's nest.

Due to its proximity to Saigon and the American Tan Son Nhut Air Base, the 25th Infantry Division moved into the area and constructed a base camp at Cu Chi, which became their headquarters. There, they built an array of fire support bases, and a signal facility on top of Nui Ba Den (Black Virgin Mountain). They also built smaller base camps at Tay Ninh and Dau Tieng that were approximately seven to ten miles from the Cambodian border.

The VC were famous for conducting an assault or ambush and retreating quickly across the border into Cambodia where the U.S. Forces were forbidden.

All of the U.S. air bases, fire support bases, and base camps were constantly harassed, mostly at night by rocket attacks, a lone sniper or small arms fire. The VC would pop up out of a tunnel, fire on the base, and then disappear back into the tunnel before they were located and eliminated. Occasionally, these attacks were followed by a sapper attack or a full-ground assault.

For those of you who might think the word sapper is a typo, it is not. A NVA/VC Sapper is a Demolition Commando and his purpose is to penetrate an American defensive perimeter in advance of a ground attack. Their primary weapons of choice were multiple satchel charges. Their job was to create chaos on base, while the main infantry force conducted a major ground assault from outside the base. The end result—Americans fighting two battle-fronts at the same time.

My base camp, considered medium in size, was pretty much round in shape and the perimeter protected by concertina wire in front of a line of bunkers. Within the wire, we had claymore mines, controlled by the bunker guards, and trip flares. Once tripped, the flares gave notice of enemy encroachment of the perimeter.

On dark moonless nights, overcast weather or during heavy rain, the VC would enter the perimeter wire and attempt to locate the trip flares and use rubber bands to prevent the flares from being tripped. Their motive—preparation for a later day assault, with a much larger force and not having to slow down for trip flares.

Undeterred by the flares, they could quickly get a man with an RPG rocket launcher close enough to a bunker to put a round into the window, destroying the bunker and giving them a sure, unchallenged entrance onto the base. Once that happened, it was total chaos.

That happened only twice during my tour.

Over the years, I have kept in touch with two of my squad members. One lives in Washington state and the other in Pennsylvania. Five years ago, they traveled to Florida with their wives and spent a week with me. I took them on an offshore charter in the Gulf of Mexico and an inshore fishing trip in Lemon Bay. We shared some great food and drinks at local restaurants and had some lengthy conversations about the last forty years.

The three of us have always had a very strong bond because of our experiences together in Vietnam. The funny thing is, during the entire week, not one of us brought up the subject of that time in our lives.

My wife later said that she thought that was odd. She was not there and will never be able to comprehend what we experienced or the bonds we formed.

War is an ugly business that scars your heart and soul forever.

Footnote from Ron Brooks:

During the war there were 180 miles of tunnels, some built directly under the 25th Infantry Command Post. Today, Cu Chi is now Viet Cong Disneyland, Vietnam's most popular attraction. Tourist can fire AK-47s or M-16s for $1.50 a round. Black pajamas are made to order on the spot, and Ho Chi Minh sandals go for $8.00.

MY GHOST

by Patrick McCrary

Herbert Hoover once said, "Older men declare war but it is the youth that must fight and die." There is no doubt that it is a true statement. I know many men have experienced the horrors of war throughout the history of our great country. Unfortunately, to know these horrors well, one must have been there. I've been there and I can say war is in no one's best interest and not for the weak of heart. You must do without the necessities of life. Hunt or be hunted like an animal, in a state of total exhaustion. The only thing that keeps you going is your adrenaline and the instinct to stay alive.

It is impossible to put on paper the exhaustion, the adrenaline, the elements and the enemy. Combat is total terror and ultimate confusion, mixed with death. It is knowing one must follow the orders issued regardless of the risk—no discussion, no question—only mindless obedience. I am a Marine, proud to serve.

Walking the "point," that's the first man in the column, is a dangerous position. Some point man duties rated better than others, depending on where you were and through which areas. No one ever volunteered to walk the point. It was the squad leader's responsibility to keep track of whose turn it was.

I was the squad leader for the 2nd Squad, 2nd Platoon A Company 1/5, 1st Marine Division. On January 25, 1969, our platoon left bridge security duties and took up flanking positions for a team of Marine combat engineers assigned the daily task of keeping the road to An Hoa clear of mines.

When we reached our objective, a trail that forked off the main road, our commander directed me to take my squad on point to the area we would be patrolling for the next few days.

I said to Lance Corporal Sanford Close Jr., "Close, you got the point. Move us outta here."

"It's not my point," he replied.

His response really pissed me off. "All right," I said. "You tell me whose turn it is."

Close then said, "I don't know how you can do this. I walked point on a patrol yesterday."

I thought to myself how all of us had taken a turn at point that day, over and over. We had done sweeps and patrols, and even a daylight ambush the day before. I then barked, "You've got the point, Close. Move us outta here."

"But it's not my turn," he protested.

"You move this platoon or get yer ass to the rear of the column, NOW," I ordered.

In stunned silence, Sanford turned and started down the trail.

I waited until my radioman came and took my place in the column to direct our movements. We had covered only about 100 meters when Lance Corporal Sanford Close Jr., USMC, lost his life to a goddamed booby trap that nearly blew his legs off.

At 19 years of age, we have so many plans. Unless we are at war, unless we must take an order, unless we must give one. Those factors change the outcome of life as sure as the weaving of fate.

On January 25, 1969, I was the key that unlocked the door to Sanford's fate.

There were many deaths in our platoon. However, Sanford's touched me the deepest.

His young handsome face, his desire to live and return home to be with his girl and family, all his hopes and dreams were somehow transferred to me that day.

It took me three trips to "The Wall" before I was able to approach it, touch it, and finally, locate the name of the hero I had known. I am honored to remember someone who fell in battle, mortally wounded, who put his life above all else in defense of his country so we may breathe freely. Even today, he is always with me.

I feel as though we all carry a ghost within us. Sanford Close Jr., Lance Corporal, United States Marine Corps, shall always be mine. I will carry him with pride.

He was my friend.

In Washington DC, there is a monument known simply as "The Wall." There, on Panel #34W Line# 74, you will find Sanford. Touch his name and tell him, "Thank you." He will hear you.

THE LAST LETTER HOME

by Rita Walker

Uncle Ronnie was my mom's youngest brother, only seven years my senior, and always like a big brother, dad, and best friend rolled into one. He made a point of spending time with me, taking me bowling or to the drive-in theatre. He was my hero even before he joined the Army. Prior to his leaving for Vietnam, he came to Clermont Elementary to see me. Someone from the front office called me out of class.

Approaching the office, I saw him standing there in his uniform. He wanted to talk to me, so we went out to the playground and sat on the swings. He told me he was leaving for a place called Vietnam. I was just a child and didn't understand why he had to go, but it felt like it was something he not only had to do, but also wanted to do. I didn't comprehend how far away or how long he would be gone, but I trusted the one making the decision.

This was the last time I recall seeing him alive.

Ronnie graduated from Groveland High School in 1961, already showing signs of dedication and leadership. He was senior class vice president and secretary, president of the Beta Club, and a delegate to Boys State. He also lettered in basketball, baseball, and football.

Although he had already been accepted at Florida State University, Uncle Ronnie decided he wanted to jump out of airplanes instead. He became an Army Special Forces Green Beret Combat Engineer. It was no surprise he was selected for a Special Forces assignment because he was *special* and intended to make the military his career.

Almost twenty-two years old, Specialist Ronald Sefton Gaffney, a paratrooper and advisor on guerrilla operations, served his third tour in Vietnam and was a short timer. At the Vung Ro Bay incident on February 19, 1965, the last day of a critical three-day battle, he gave all he had left to give.

The allies recovered from a 130-foot North Vietnamese ship, 100 tons of Soviet and Chinese-made war material, including 3500 to 4000 rifles and submachine guns, one million rounds of small arms ammunition, 1500 grenades, 200 mortar rounds, and 500 pounds of explosives. The incident at Vung Ro led to the creation of the Operation Market Time coastal surveillance program.

During this time, Uncle Ronnie was serving in the role of an advisor to the South Vietnamese Army. Already wounded, he received the fatal bullet while rescuing two wounded South Vietnamese soldiers in the Phu Yen Province of South Vietnam.

For his bravery and sacrifice, he earned the Bronze Star for meritorious service while on duty. He was also awarded the Purple Heart, the National Defense Medal, the Vietnam Service Medal, and the Vietnam Campaign Medal.

On February 12, exactly one week prior to his death, Ronnie wrote in his last letter home that if he didn't make it back, only God would know why. The letter made the headlines in the *Orlando Sentinel*. Below is the portion of the letter that was printed:

I only hope they will start letting us do a little more of the fighting without waiting for the VC (Viet Cong). The town they hit Saturday, Pleiku, was the same place I was at my first trip over here. From what I hear, they slipped right up on the barracks.

Things have seemed to pick up all over the country with a great deal pointed at the Americans. I'm going to stay away from the big towns where Americans are at as much as possible and take my chances out here. Things are good where I'm at anyway and we haven't had any trouble.

I still don't want you to worry about me, for all we can do is trust in God and if I should have anything happen to me, He would be the only one who knew why.

Vietnam is very personal to me and so are the men and women who served there. Vung Ro Bay made it personal. I was fourteen, but I remember as if it happened yesterday. It changed who I was and who I am, like all the men and women who served.

Ronnie's name is on Panel 1E, Line 93, RONALD S GAFFNEY, at the Vietnam Veterans Memorial Wall in Washington DC.

In 2011, the Lake County ROTC unit

honored him as a member of the honor table.

In 2015, on the 50th anniversary of his death, the Florida Legislature designated a portion of SR 50 as Specialist Ronald Gaffney Memorial Highway.

In his memory, the City of Groveland has named a 7.6 acre park, scheduled to open in early 2017, the *Ronald Sefton Gaffney Memorial Park.* The city's website says, "Specialist Ronald Sefton Gaffney gave his young life in the service of his country, selflessly trying to save the lives of two foreign soldiers and sadly becoming the only Groveland, Florida casualty of the Vietnam War."

Fellow Vietnam Vet Tom Wedge wrote in memoriam to Ronnie, " 'We few, we happy few, we band of brothers, for he today who sheds his blood with me, shall [always] be my brother.' So Rest in Peace my brother." Origin: William Shakespeare play *Henry V.*

EPILOGUE

by James Faris

Yes, these men were brave. The real
definition of bravery is to overcome fear
and act anyway. They demonstrated that.
They answered their nation's call when
many refused, became career students,
used their political pull to get deferments,
or a slot in the reserves. Nothing about
that should denigrate today's National
Guard and Reserve. They deploy again and
again to war zones. Now they join because
they want to serve, at the risk of their own
lives.

These stories needed to be told and then
read by anyone in a position to commit our
young people to a conflict—that's anyone
who votes. Many don't know much about

this war. They should. It's been said to not understand the lessons of history dooms us to repeat our mistakes.

And we just did.

Was it a just war? The young men who wrote these stories weren't in any position to question whether it was or wasn't. The Constitution says the civilian leadership makes that decision. I had a career NCO in my command, a good man who served his country in two wars. He answered that question this way: "This might not be a good war but it's the only war we have." Yeah, a bit of gallows humor but what do we expect? We were asking him to die for us.

For the most part it was a young man's war. Fought by eighteen-year olds, led by twenty-two-year olds. Men like the ones who wrote these stories. Draftees mostly, or else like me, they joined with the draft on their heels. Like jumping into the flames to avoid getting burned. Many senior officers and NCOs found ways to keep out of harm's way. Although not all and during the TET offensive there was nowhere safe.

Before going overseas, they displayed the false bravado young men do when they are scared. When they marched in training, they sang what we called "Jody Cadence." One line haunts me to this day: "I want to be an airborne ranger, I want to live a life of danger, I want to go to Vietnam." The refrain ends with: "Box me up and send me home."

There was no way for them to hide what they were when they returned. Civilian clothes didn't disguise the fact they were soldiers—or had been. If the haircuts didn't give it away, they no longer dressed the same way. Their shoes shined, shirts pressed and tucked, their gig lines straight. (If the reader doesn't know what a gig line is, ask a vet.)

Even some veterans' groups turned their backs. At first the VFW refused to recognize them because they didn't view this as a war—VFW stands for Veterans of Foreign Wars. The American Legion did not, God bless them.

Imagine what a shock it was for a young man to come home after facing death and seeing his friends die next to him to be subjected to the scorn of those who didn't approve of the war and the arrogance of those who found ways to sit it out. No one who hadn't been through what they had understands how so much of what people worry about back here is trivial compared to having their lives and those of their comrades on the line every day.

It was an honor to help edit these stories. It brought back old memories. Not all of them bad. Someone said rather than say "Thank you for your service" we should say "Welcome home." It's time to do that now for these men.

James Faris, 1LT Armor, U.S. Army 1966-1969

If you enjoyed my book, please go to Amazonbooks.com and write a review. You must state you bought the book from the author or they will not post because they did not sell it to you

Thank you, The Author

CLASSMATES
WHO SERVED IN VIETNAM

Larry Allen Class of 1968
Mike Allen Class of 1966
John Black Class of 1965
Robin Bon-Jorn Class of 1962
Kenny Boykin Class of 1958
Terry Brown Class of 1968
Ronnie Brooks Class of 1968
Paul Bruno Class of 1963
John Bumbalough Class of 1963
Mike Butler Class of 1965
Richard Cole Class of 1966
Ted Cook Class of 1966
Marion Craig Class of 1964
Charles Driggs Class of 1963
Earl Futch Class of 1966
David Gaines Class of 1964
Bill Gehlback Class of 1960
Philip Gray Class of 1967
Jay Harris Class of 1960 (Howey Academy)
Gary Heath Class of 1965
Eddie Hull Class of 1960
David Engersol Class of 1967
David Jarvis Class of 1962
Bobby Jones Class of 1966
Danny Jones Class of 1963

Oscar Kennedy
Joe Koester Class of 1959
Sammy Lane Class of 1965
Nicky Lindsey Class of 1964
John Macdonald Class of 1967
Michael McCrary
Patrick McCrary
Stan Oliver Class of 1965
Paul Rester Class of 1964
David Rieman Class of 1964
Charles (Buddy) Rountree Class of 1966
John Rountree
Tom Sangster Class of 1966
D. C. Steorts Class of 1967
Jimmy Skipper Class of 1969
Chris St. John Class of 1968
Kent Swanson Class of 1970
Chuck Taylor Class of 1967
Troy Taylor
Duanne Thomas Class of 1966
Butch Tully Class of 1966
Roger Williams Class of 1968
Terry Vandermeer Class of 1968

Please note: All classmates who served in Vietnam may not be included. Our list is only as accurate as the information provided by fellow classmates. If your name or a loved one's name is missing, we sincerely apologize.

MEMORIAL

LEST THEY BE FORGOTTEN

Class of 1963

John Bumbalough
Charles Driggs

Class of 1964

Marion Craig
David Gaines
Nicky Lindsey

Class of 1966

Richard Cole
Chuck Taylor
Duanne Thomas
Butch Tully

Class of 1967

Philip Gray

CONTRIBUTING AUTHORS' BIOS

Joseph Robin Bon-Jorn

Born in Chicago, Illinois, Joseph, better known as Robin, moved to Clermont when he was five. He graduated from Clermont High School in 1962 and enlisted in 1964. Unsure which branch of service he should join, he asked his friend, Brenda Moore. She said she liked the marine uniforms the best, so he joined the Marines.

While stationed in Hawaii, Robin called his high school sweetheart, Susan Bourquin, and asked her if she wanted to get married. Robin became a father to Susan's daughter, Kecia. Together Robin and Susan had two more children, Christian and Trampis.

Following his divorce from Susan, Robin married Pamela Williams in 1981. Pam had two children Eric and Eve and they became a family of seven.

Robin, an adventurous guy, loves the outdoors and has boated the Florida and Bahamas coasts. He has also fished almost every lake, gulf and ocean waters in Florida. Robin loves guns and even owns a gun shop. He truly believes he is the happiest and luckiest person ever.

Paul Bruno

Paul was born October 8, 1945 at Waterman Hospital, Leesburg, Florida to Ruby and Dominick Bruno. He moved to Clermont when he was in first grade and graduated 1963. While attending high school, he worked at Publix Super Market.

After graduation, he worked briefly for a gold mining company in Dahlonega, Georgia. When that didn't pan out, he returned to Clermont and went to work at Konsler Steel. Eight months later, he was transferred to the engineering office, which fed his desire to further his education. He enrolled in college and while there, he met his future wife, Judith Fleming, from Winter Garden, Florida. They married June 17, 1967.

Six months after their marriage, Paul received his draft notice. In lieu of being drafted, he joined the Navy. During his time in the Navy, he served fourteen months aboard the Navy destroyer USS STRIBLING that included a tour of Vietnam. He spent the last month of his Navy service in Charleston, South Carolina, where he was later discharged for medical reasons.

Paul returned to Clermont and went back to work at what was now Williams

Steel. Six months later, he went to work at Thompson Welding in Astatula, Florida, as head of the engineering department. Two and a half years later, he started his own engineering company, Custom Drafting & Design, Inc.

Over the next forty years, his company prepared engineering drawings for thousands of buildings in central Florida and the east coast states. Paul and his wife, Judy, retired in 2012 and now live in Zellwood, Florida. They have three children: Dominick, Alisa, and Benjamin.

Ted Cook

Ted Cook, given name Oscar Theodore, was born in Kansas City, Missouri, 1948. He moved to Clermont, Florida, in 1955 and started third grade and graduated high school in 1966. After a year at Lake Sumter Junior College, he joined the Army in late spring of 1967.

Before going to Vietnam, Ted spent a year in Washington DC. He served in Nam from January 1969 until September of 1970. Upon returning stateside, he enrolled at Seminole Junior College in January 1971. Three years later, he transferred to University of South Florida where he earned a degree in chemistry.

In 1978, he found a job with an analytical instrument company and moved to Germantown (Memphis), Tennessee, where he met his wife, Cynthia Kay. They were married for 29 years. No kids, but since they were Humane Society volunteers, lots of critters.

Ted retired early when Kay passed away in 2011.

In 2013, he moved to Fayetteville, Arkansas, where he works part-time as an analyst for an environmental lab and as a research associate in a statewide Mass Spectrometry Lab at the University of Arkansas.

Jay Harris

Born in Chicago in 1941, Jay moved to Clermont in 1955, where he completed the ninth grade. He then attended Bowles Military Academy and Howey Academy. After graduating in 1960, he attended college for three years before joining the U.S. Air Force in 1963.

Following basic training at Amarillo, Texas, Jay was assigned to Myrtle Beach Air Force Base. In 1966, he volunteered for a tour in Vietnam. He was stationed at Binh Thuy Air Base near Can Tho, in the Mekong Delta area of South Vietnam where he served for one year.

In 1967, Jay returned stateside, worked for Martin Marietta for several years in the Orlando and Ocala areas, and completed his degree in business. Later, he was employed by Florida Telephone and following a series of mergers ended up with Sprint in charge of Logistics and Procurement. Jay retired in 2007, lived in Eustis for several years and now resides in Tavares. Married and divorced, he has two sons, Jamie and Jason.

Bob Jones

Bob was born in Washington, Indiana, in 1948 and moved to Clermont in 1960. He enlisted in the Marine Corps out of high school in 1966 and shipped out to Vietnam in 1967. He spent thirteen months in Nam and felt blessed to return home in one piece.

In 1968, he married Tiffany Middleton and a year later started college and received his AA degree. After college, Bob started working in his family's watermelon business.

In 2003, Bob and Tiffany started their own company, Jones & Jones Enterprises. They have two children, a son, Matt, and a daughter named Dallas. Currently, their son and daughter are partners in the business.

Joe Koester

Born in Charleston, WV, Joe moved to Clermont when he was 13, graduated Class of 1959, and joined the U.S. Air Force in 1960. Joe trained as an intelligence analyst and served at Anchorage, AK, Shemya Island in the western Aleutians, and at Misawa Air Base in Northern Japan. He served four years, four months and one day.

He was employed by the National Security Agency in the Washington DC area in April, 1966, and subsequently volunteered for a position in support of the J2 (Intelligence) of MACV Headquarters and completed a tour in Vietnam between March 1969 and March 1970. Joe served as an intelligence analyst responsible for I Corps (Northern South Vietnam) and supported primarily Army and Marine Corps forces in the north. Joe received NSA's Meritorious Civilian Service Award in 1982.

He retired from NSA in December 1998, moved to Tennessee in January 1999 and enjoyed retirement until 9/11, when he volunteered to return to NSA and worked there until March 2002. Later, he received a request to assist the U.S. Army at Fort Gordon, Georgia, and worked until our forces took Baghdad in April 2003.

Joe married his high school prom date from his junior year, Katherine Arey from Montverde. In his my spare time he collects and restores antique radios, and is an Amateur Radio (HAM) Operator, call sign W4NSA.

John Macdonald

Born and raised in Clermont, John graduated in 1967. Following graduation, he worked at Winn Dixie until he received his draft notice in July 1969. He went active duty December 1969 and did a tour in Vietnam. Afterwards, he returned stateside and was stationed at Fort Riley, Kansas. He spent six weeks in Germany and participated in Reforger Maneuvers. Before being discharged in 1972, he married Jonlen, whom he had met while stationed in Kansas. John received an Honorable Discharge and a Commendation Medal for good job and character.

After serving his country, John and his wife settled in Orlando. John worked for Winn Dixie September '72-73 and went to night school to learn skills to become a Journeyman Carpenter.

He worked as a carpenter from 1973 to 1980. December 1980 to December 1981, he attended a vocational school to become a dental technician and worked in a dental office from December 1981 to March 1983. Earning a degree in Dental Lab Technology and a certified dental technician, he taught at Southern College from March 1983 to April 2001. Then he went to work for Global Prosthetics. He worked there from April 2001 until he retired April 2011.

John and wife raised two sons, Jeff, a manager with Olive Garden and Jason, a professional dancer in New York City. In August 2013, John and Jonlen relocated back to Clermont. They enjoy boating, camping, road trips and movies. John still enjoys carpentry, building Cat Trees for their four adorable kittens. John has become known as the 'Catman'.

Michael McCrary

Michael was born at the South Lake Memorial Hospital in Clermont in June of 1948. He attended Clermont High School from 1961 to 1965. At the end of his sophomore year and only seventeen years old, he volunteered to join the Navy.

During his four years in the service, he sailed to twenty-six countries and took advantage of his many shore leaves, which allowed him to experience what other countries were like.

Returning from Nam in 1965, Michael drove trucks locally for about fifteen years. In 1980 and for the next twenty-five years, he was a long-distance driver. Michael is married and lives in Clermont.

Patrick McCrary

Born in Clermont, Florida, Patrick joined the U.S. Marine Corps on his eighteenth birthday July 9, 1967. He reported to Boot Camp at Parris Island, South Carolina, August 31, 1967 and on January 31, 1968 left the United States headed to Vietnam. On February 6, 1968, he landed in Da Nang, South Vietnam. Trained as a rifleman, he served his full-time in Vietnam as a combat Marine.

McCrary was awarded the Purple Heart for wounds received on August 3, 1968. He left Vietnam on February 22, 1969 and upon his return stateside, he was stationed at Parris Island, South Carolina, where he advanced to the rank of sergeant.

June 10, 1970, he was granted an Honorable Discharge and returned to Clermont to start his life as an adult. Jobs near impossible in his hometown, he moved to Pensacola, Florida, in January of 1971 and where he remains to this day.

Patrick attended college on the GI Bill, and worked several dead end jobs until finding his niche with the United States Postal Service. He retired from the postal service with 27 years of service. Married three times, he fathered two sons and in his golden years still yearns to return to Clermont.

Kent Swanson

The second of three children, Kent was born in Brockton, Massachusetts, in July of 1952. Six weeks later, the family moved to Lockport, Illinois, where his dad worked as a welding inspector at the caterpillar factory in Joliet. When Kent started first grade they moved to Clermont, Florida.

Kent graduated from Clermont High School in 1970 and attended Augustana College in Rock Island, Illinois, with a declared major of physics. At the end of two years, he married his high school sweetheart and joined the Air Force. He spent 1974 being a target in the Vietnam War.

After serving his country for four years, he returned to Florida and attended the University of Central Florida (then called

Florida Technological University) where he graduated as a physicist. For the next fourteen years, he worked at Martin Marietta designing weapon systems for the government. Later, he went into working for himself—remodeling homes.

Kent retired at 59 and now enjoys his passions and hobbies that include traveling, mountain hiking, motorcycling and spending time with his new wife, Ruth, and their many children and grandchildren.

Ruth Robinson/Swanson

In June of 1952, Ruth was born in Philadelphia, Pennsylvania, and graduated with honors in 1970 from Clermont High School. Her late husband, William J. Robinson aka Bill Robinson, served in the Army for two years 1969 to 1971, most of which was in-country in Vietnam and Cambodia. They were married for 37 years before he died. Together, they raised eight children and lived in Bagdad, Arizona, for seven years before moving to Clermont.

After moving to Clermont where Ruth grew up, Bill worked at Florida Crushed Stone and Jhana Mines. In the early years, Bill had a country music band and played in Las Vegas, Nevada, and Bagdad, Arizona. When they moved to Clermont, he could be found singing and playing his guitar at events sponsored by the sand mines. Playing music brought him comfort and purpose.

In the year 2000, he was diagnosed with PTSD and granted Total Disability. Bill stopped playing his music.

Ruth retired from Walt Disney after 18 years in 2001 to be his full-time caregiver. For the next few years, the couple traveled across the United States until Bill's health and state of mind no longer permitted them to do so.

After her husband's death in 2011, Ruth started college at the age of 59, graduating with an Associate in Office Administration and Computer Applications in 2013. Then as fate would have it, she reunited with her childhood friend, Kent Swanson. They are now married and live in Orlando, Florida. Ruth and Kent are presently enjoying the "dessert phase" of their lives, traveling across the USA, exploring new places as well as visiting family and friends.

Rita Walker

Rita Walker, niece of Ronald Gaffney who submitted a beautiful tribute to her uncle, was born and raised in Clermont. She graduated in 1969 and couldn't wait to move away, but like a homing pigeon, she made a full circle back home.

Rita married young, trained as a medical assistant and worked mostly in the medical field until retiring as a medical office manager. Rita and her husband have three children and seven grandchildren.

Her uncle, who graduated from Groveland High School and lost his life in Vietnam, is believed to be the only causality within our surrounding area.

Marsha McAllister Partlow

Marsha graduated from Clermont High School with the Class of 1965 and attended Asbury College in Wilmore, Kentucky. Upon graduating from college in 1969, she served in Jamaica and West Indies as a Peace Corps volunteer from June 1969 until September 1972.

In 1984, Marsha earned a Master's Degree in the Teaching of Adult Education from Alaska Pacific University, Anchorage. For several years in the '90s, she was the State of Alaska Director of Adult Education and most recently Coordinator for Catholic Community Service in Juneau, Alaska.

One year ago, 2016, Marsha returned to the Clermont area and attended a meeting where she volunteered to help a group of veterans write their stories. She recorded four men and one woman's versions of their experiences. Once satisfied with their accounts, she wrote them down and forwarded to Mary Collins Brown, who with the help of her critique group converted Marsha's efforts and the recordings into five remarkable stories. The recitations she recorded were from Bobby Jones, Michael McCrary, Rita Walker, Jay Harris and Ron Brooks. Without her help and added effort there might not have been enough stories to make *We Were Brave* a reality.

Marsha is the proud mother of two daughters and five grandchildren.

Mary Collins Brown

Mary was born in Kentucky and moved to Clermont the middle of her seventh grade year. She graduated in 1964 and attended Appalachian State, Boone, North Carolina. In 1967, she married Rodney Brown, Class of 1961. Over the next few years, due to Rodney's employment in the construction end of building motels, they lived in Savannah, Georgia, Tampa, Florida, Birmingham, Alabama, and Memphis, Tennessee. In 1974, they settled in the Florida Panhandle where Rodney established his own construction company. Mary worked by his side while raising four children, dabbling in retail and pursuing her writing.

Mary became actively involved in a local writers' group in 2002, served four years as Treasurer and Board Member, and presently is the chairperson of a long-running critique group. Her love of writing began at age twelve when she moved from Kentucky to Florida, touching loved ones she left behind with her heartfelt letters. Her father encouraged Mary to pursue writing while attending college; however, life happened and only during the last several years has she been able to devote herself to the art.

Writing has sustained Mary through many trials and tribulations, imparting emotions her readers can relate to, which is why her business card reads: Writing from the Heart...Her first novel *Remember the Rose* invokes the message: No matter how beautiful the rose or how sweet its fragrance, its thorns can inflict pain. Her second novel *Waiting for the Daffodils* delves on the omen: Legend foretells a single daffodil brings misfortune...

Through her own personal writing, Mary has gained peace and insight, and the reason she decided to tackle putting together the collection of short stories for the men of Clermont who served in

Vietnam. Her wish is that all the contributors can finally be at peace for whatever they had to do to stay alive.

Made in the USA
Columbia, SC
07 April 2018